Beyond the Veil

INNER VISIONS SERIES #9

Beyond the Veil

Amazing descriptions of life after death and the surprising world which awaits us all!

Judy Laddon

PLUS: Twenty people's lives evaluated from the other side

First Edition published by
Lawrence Shook Communications

International Standard Book Number 0-917086-97-X

Cover Design and Illustrations by Leslie W. LePere

Printed in the United States of America

Published by ACS Publications, Inc.
P.O. Box 16430
San Diego, CA 92116-0430

Dedication
A book dedicated to Judy Laddon by an entity called Af

Contents

Part
One

BEYOND THE VEIL

Messages from "beyond" describe the
meaning and purpose of life and the
reality of the afterlife.

Introduction

MANY people who pick up this book won't believe in me, the author. For I am not Judy Laddon, who takes down my words and faithfully types them up each day, in order to create an organized manuscript. I bring my words into her mind, but they are not hers. I am what you would call a spirit, or even a ghost. Yet I am more lively and less ghostly than you can imagine! I am an entity living in the vast realms of the universe, and I know of your realm—your Earth—and of each of you. I treasure your world and I wish to help you.

Throughout history there have been people who have communed with so-called spirits. You may be vaguely aware of them. In ancient and biblical times there were prophets, seers and oracles. Mystics had visions and "out-of-body" experiences. If the validity of these events had not been accepted by a good number of people, then today we, or rather you on Earth, would have no religions to speak of. That the established religions of the West today do not accept paranormal events as valid occurrences of people who are connected with the universe is a contradiction in terms. These religions were born out of such experiences. To believe in God and a realm of God—or spirit existing apart from the physical—is to admit that we are all connected. The spiritual and the physical are intimately tied.

So as you begin to read this book, do not discount the possible reality of its unearthly author. We are not, however, attempting to encourage gullibility. I suggest only that the reader keep an open mind, as does my secretary Judy Laddon. I am called upon to reassure her that the voice she hears in her head is not her own. It is not her subconscious bubbling forth. It is my voice, and I have chosen to speak to your world through her. She is not, by the way, a saintly type, nor is she religious at all in the way that term is understood. She could be called an ordinary person. She has three children, a devoted husband with whom she enjoys a spirited and earthly relationship, and at the time we write these words she has a regular job.

This information is given as backgound so that the readers of this modest narrative understand its nature and the manner in which it came to be expressed. When I say Ms. Laddon is ordinary, I do so to make a point. The accepted measures of personal worth and distinction in your society are distorted, bringing with them much pain, disillusionment and sorrow.

I give to you the advice I have given to Judy: You should keep an open heart and a clear mind. The open heart is to be understanding of your fellow human beings, and of assistance to them whenever you can be. The clear mind is to be able to hear the urgings of your own intuitions, for these bring the greatest truths you will know in this lifetime.

Your experiences all happen for a purpose. This is an important lesson and one which few in your society have learned or intuited. There are no accidents in this universe. Naturally, most people are unaware of the truths underlying apparent accidents. These often relate to a person's previous life experiences. So now we must mention the unmentionable, reincarnation. I don't understand why there is public sentiment against such a natural occurrence. The shape of a person's evolution goes simply like this: A consciousness is born. It has gathered enough strength to thrust itself into the world. Most often, physical life offers such a wealth of learning potential that the personality enters into a long series of incarnations. The spirit moves in and out of the flesh countless times. The value of physical life is unique. It offers opportunities for freedom, freedom to regress as well as progress, freedom to stretch out in all directions and explore all possibilities; and all of this is a rich learning experience for the personality, the soul.

Now, we "up here" have heard over and over again the same sorry lament: "If there is a God in heaven, then why do such terrible things happen on Earth?" My answer is this. People have been given the freedom to direct their own fate. This is a gift from God in itself. This freedom is the truest expression of their nature, but it also means that humankind has the freedom to make mistakes and to do wrong. Who is God to prevent such an experience? "However," I hear you say, "what about innocent victims?" To that I answer that if anyone is innocent, then all people are innocent, even the criminals who are innocently ignorant of the true purposes of life and their own grave misconceptions. By the same token, so-called victims are not truly innocents caught in hapless accidents. If you only understood the intricate web of psychological underpinning which is the birthright of every human being, many of these mysteries would become clear.

All humans are ageless. The young child or babe in arms is as ancient as the stars. That life, the consciousness, is eternal and can never be destroyed.

People choose their own life circumstances. If you were in my realm, you would witness the countless members who eagerly await an opportunity to be born into your system. They cherish and yearn for the joys and the rich environment which they will find there. And for many, the realm of spirit, which is rich in lessons of its own, cannot substitute for the earthly experience.

No doubt this information will sound shocking to many. "Could it possibly be true?" you ask. It goes against all the accepted ideas about life which exist within the cultural fabric of your society. Babies do not choose to be born, you think. They just happen to be born. But that simply isn't true.

Babies are full-fledged and fully developed spirits, who appear to others in an adult form in the realm of spirit. And if their souls urge them to seek further lessons on the Earth plane, then they study and search for the right circumstances in which to make an entrance. They look for a mother—often they carefully watch women who are already expecting—and they get entered on a kind of cosmic waiting list. These births are watched over carefully by many in my realm, and the most appropriate matches are sought out. And so the baby is not a newcomer to your world but probably as old as his or her parents. That is one reason parents find they can learn much from their progeny.

5

The essential point here is to indicate the strength and power of consciousness. Consciousness creates the body, not vice versa. The existence of the body does not create the soul; it is foolish to assume that is the case. The body is only so much meat. The brain is a vacuous organ, a mass of lifeless tissue, without a willing spirit to enter it and breathe life, vitality and thought into it.

"Your thoughts are a definition of yourself and your growth."

This baby enters her circumstances for a particular reason. There are portions of the character she wishes to flesh out, so to speak. Perhaps she has had problems in the past with being overly proud, intolerant of other people. She might choose to be born into a family which experiences poverty, in order to learn humility. Perhaps the soul has, in previous lives, discriminated against others of contrasting nationality, race or gender. Then she may choose to be born into a minority race, in order to experience from the other side the injustices which she was guilty of imposing upon others. Perhaps a soul has been physically violent or cruel in a previous life. She may choose circumstances or experiences which will bring home the full implications of past actions. This is, of course, the Eastern idea of karma. An eye for an eye, literally, to balance the scales of justice. But in every case, the judge, the person who makes the final judgment and punishment, is the individual herself. You have created your own circumstances. This is one of the greatest lessons you can learn in this life, and if you can accept it, your further lessons can be very fulfilling.

There are several dangers, though, in accepting fully the truth of these statements or laws. First of all, many would then conclude that they are victims of a past they do not remember, and pawns to this greater mystery. This is the truth: you are no pawn, and you create your own life from moment to moment. The impetus is within your mind. Your strength towers above all the mountains of your Earth: it lies in your thoughts. Thoughts are the womb of your world. They give birth to all the events which comprise your life. Your thoughts are a definition of yourself and your growth. They can delay your spiritual progress or rush you onward as fast as you please.

While many events happen to you of which you had no conscious thought, still you must not underestimate the power of your conscious thoughts. You all have a greater psyche, or soul, which is in touch with your spirit history. On this greater level many of the events which find physical expression are first formulated, but they respond unfailingly to the conscious mind. When an important lesson has been absorbed by you and is reflected in your thinking, then extraordinary measures are not taken to teach that lesson. But if many subtle efforts have been urged upon a person and have been rejected, then more forceful means may be taken in order to teach essential lessons.

It is most important to understand, above all, that life on your planet and, in fact, all existence throughout the universe—and it is more abundant than you can guess—has great meaning. It is watched over by the gods. There are countless souls who are caretakers of every aspect of your world, and you each are surrounded by more love than I can describe. So feel secure; the world has purpose and its purposes are good.

I spoke of the dangers of misunderstanding karma. One is this: Many will say, "OK, if that person was meant to suffer, then why should I interfere?" This might be used as an excuse against helping the needy who surround you. This is a mistake. While it is true that there are no innocent victims in this life, it is also important for each person to learn compassion for others and to develop a sympathetic desire to help others who are in situations of need. Perhaps this is the greatest lesson of all, that the true nature of spirit, which lies within each of you, struggles to grow wise and, in so doing, struggles to understand

7

others and help them in their growth. We are all a community of spirits; we belong together.

Since we are all connected within the universe, it is only natural for there to be a connectedness of thought from our realm to yours. You have only temporarily left the spirit realm to experience physical life. Too, you participate in this realm on levels of which you are consciously unaware. The dreaming state is one example. Sleep, for the most part, is a mystery to you. From our side we are aware of its necessary function. During sleep people are tied into their whole selves or psyches, and truths are revealed to them. It is a time for learning and remembering lessons past. It is more therapeutic than your behavioral scientists imagine, and it is essential to mental health and a feeling of emotional wholeness. Much intuitive wisdom is transferred during sleep states to an area of the brain where it is available to the conscious, waking mind. In this manner help is offered from our world to yours in a natural process.

Now, my secretary Judy has a nagging question which she feels should be included at this point. I had not planned to interject it here, but to clear her mind and assuage her editor's bent, I will address it. Why is it that humankind is born without conscious knowledge of a greater psyche, a history of incarnations, intimate connections to the rest of the universe? The answer is partly obvious. To recall previous incarnations would make one's focus in this life extremely difficult—in fact, impossible. There have simply been too many lives prior to the current one.

But let me add this. There have been human cultures where the relationship between people and the spirits around them was much more apparent. In other societies in the past and in certain present cultures, the role of the intuitions and "occult" knowledge and perceptions are taken seriously. In these societies much universal truth is thereby gained.

Even so, there are sometimes problems in the translation from one realm to another, hence certain distortions or untruths are sometimes adopted along with the truths. Your own Bible is just such an example. Genuine inspiration and intuitive truths are at the foundation of much of it, but many misconceptions and falsehoods have also been adopted on a wholesale basis. A couple of important ones, for example, are:

"The idea of Hell is a misunderstanding which has caused more suffering and grief than all the criminals in all the prisons of your world."

---

1) God is to be feared, that (S)He is cruel or jealous. Such is blatantly false. Everyone of my realm has a direct perception of the Supreme Being, a single immense entity which you call God. This presence is sensed in a tangible manner all around us, and the emotional tone is one of abundant love and an expansive, supportive sympathy in every aspect of our existence.

2) The idea of Hell is a misunderstanding which has caused more suffering and grief than all the "criminals" in all the prisons of your world. There are no personalities in all the universe who are forever damned. There is no Hell as it has been taught. All life has God's blessing, and every soul, no matter how errant or mistaken his or her actions, has a hopeful future. The power lies within each person.

There is what would be considered a symbolic corollary to Hell. Those who have made grave errors on Earth choose to take difficult paths to help correct their wrongs. There are many ways to approach this, which I will be covering in the main text. For now, suffice it to say that the church's teachings of hellfire and damnation should be sent to Hell, figuratively, and never heard from again.

One other point about the conscious mind, in order to satisfy Ms. Laddon's questionings. There is a great purpose to your lack of remembering the realities from whence you spring. This amnesia is an integral part of the human experience. Humans are meant to take themselves seriously. Human life is a great and noble process; it holds tremendous potential as a learning tool. It's a kind of test for each individual. If you knew the test questions in advance, you might not absorb the lessons of the exam to the fullest, correct? In this analogy, one would be able to cram for the exam, perhaps not fully comprehending the subject. The same is true in life. To absorb all the lessons of life, it is best for people to be focused on one life alone, without preconceptions from this side or forced information that hasn't been fully absorbed.

Earth is the testing ground, and it is a magnificent one. You are all there by choice, and the Earth is created by you, in concert with the greater scope of the universe, for your joy and your fulfillment. On that note, let us move on to the main subject of this book: the realm of the spirit.

1 Death of the Body

I SHOULD make one more comment before embarking on an imaginary, though typical, journey into the unknown realm of the spirit. That is to mention the reasons for doing so. It is clear to me that the many troubles which plague your planet and its populace have sprung from human being's misconceptions about themselves and the meaning of life. Instead of me lecturing about the truths of human life, I am now choosing to reveal the larger, unseen world all around you. My idea, a good one I think, is that by so revealing the structures of spirit all about your world, many truths of your lives will automatically become clear. Since the same laws apply to all realms of consciousness, it can be practically useful for you to glimpse this world beyond. Where our experiment is successful, it will help people become oriented in a more wholesome and constructive relation to themselves, their neighbors and friends. So then, here we go.

Let's take one example at a time which illustrates a typical class of people. We will first look at what happens to a very sick person upon his death.

The body has now ceased to function and perhaps certain relatives or medical types are gathered around. The man himself, however, feels perfectly fit. In fact, he feels better than he has for a long time. The only unusual thing to him is that he finds he is floating at the top of the room, looking down upon his own dead body and his grieving family! Naturally he is surprised to find himself in such an odd position! He feels an emotional tugging both toward his now-lifeless body and toward his family, who cannot see him. He also may feel a turbulence and confusion within his mind if he did not believe in survival of the spirit while he was still living. Hopefully, this "dearly departed" will be open-minded enough to accept the fact that his body is dead and that he has still survived.

11

Just as rumor has it, there is a "silver cord" which attaches the spirit body to the physical body, and this cord is severed before our friend goes on his way. In most cases, arrangements have been made for a familiar guide to be on hand to help the newcomer adjust to his surroundings. Often this is a former friend, or a previously departed family member, who arrives on the death scene and both comforts and welcomes the new traveler.

There are countless variations on this theme. Many of you may have read instances of those who had been technically dead for a few moments, then regained life and told of vivid dreams wherein they entered a long, dark tunnel, then approached a great light and finally met a kind of celestial tribunal where they reviewed their lives and were sent back. This is not a universal experience. There are—I'm sorry to smash an accepted fantasy—no golden gates where individuals are judged and sent to an eternal fate. As you might imagine, there are certain similarities in the accounts of people who have had the experience of being near death and then regaining their health. In these cases, there is a question on our side whether the time is ripe for the individual's death. And so they are brought before a cosmic jury of sorts to determine if they should come to this side or return to Earth. In all the cases you may have read about, the individual is sent back to Earth. But this is in no way a final judgment the religious folk preach about. It is merely a kind of clearinghouse of information and concern pertaining to the individual, one of the countless examples of the supports from the spirit realm which surround each of you.

I cannot emphasize enough that there are many, many spirits, whole personalities like yourself yet without an earthly body, who surround you and are lovingly concerned with your development. And there is a wide variety of occupations for these entities on our side. There are also echelons or levels of activity. Certain decisions, especially life-or-death ones, are made only at the higher levels. Such is the case with these examples of souls returned to life. It had been judged by spirits at a high level that it would be best for the persons to return to their physical life, and so it was arranged.

In the case of the deceased in our example, no such last-minute judgment was necessary, and his transition to this side is easy and natural.

2 | Evaluation of the Life

THE self which you know is but a small, even tiny, percentage of your total personality. It is necessary to be so focused in order to most benefit by your physical life. Upon death, however, each of you has a very noticeable broadening of your faculties. It can be compared to suddenly being clairvoyant and telepathic, being able to read other people's thoughts easily. This is actually the case once you are freed of the earthly body. You can, indeed, read the thoughts of those around you. This is done without relying on language at all. Thoughts are transmitted in a wordless yet universally recognized language of the mind. Simply put, you become aware of the thoughts, emotions and overall tone of the personalities around you.

"There are many souls who wake up over here to realize that they literally missed the point of life."

Another important change occurs, a miraculous process of "awakening." In a twinkling, it becomes apparent what the main purpose was of the life just completed, and whether that purpose had been addressed. You would be amazed and saddened to see

this self-acknowledgment and self-judgment from our side. There
are many souls who "wake up" over here to realize that they literally missed the point of life.   They forgot their original purpose, they got sidetracked. This is not to say there are not many
who have been greatly fulfilled and true to their inner impetus.
But in your Western society especially we are seeing too many
arrive over here who are immediately shocked by their own
blindness during life to their greater goals.

I am not implying yours is a sick society, for it is filled with a
number of wise and intuitive souls who will help you change to
more meaningful structures. I am trying to show what we perceive to be an epidemic of disillusioned spirits who reach this
side and are unfailingly remorseful to have completely bypassed
the important tasks of their lives.   They then must labor for
many years—though time has no meaning over here—to recon-
struct their original intentions, evaluate their failings, study Earth
circumstances and enroll for another human life.

Now, this is just a small part of any person's, or entity's, endeavors on this side.   It is, though, one of the first and most
potent experiences you will have after death,   the face-to-face
encounter with your own soul and your own spiritual development.   It is such an impressive experience that many do not re-
cover their formerly blase´ attitude about fate for many lives, if
ever.   Those who have most disappointed themselves may have
the greatest drive in their next life, or the deepest passion for
achievement among their fellow men.   There always remains the
danger, however, that one can misdirect this driving force away
from one's original purpose.

Here is a simple example of how many in your system become
corrupted.   Let's say a man is born into a life with the express
purpose at the outset of developing abilities along sensitive, inter-
personal lines.   Let's say communication is a major goal for this
life.   An appropriate background might be something like this:
In a past life this personality became so disillusioned by others
that he withdrew into himself and refused to communicate any of

his ideals. He became something like a hermit, even if apparently living a normal life in society.

From this unfortunate experience, the soul might next be urged to concentrate on communicating with those around him on a dramatic scale. A position of prominence in a publishing or broadcasting firm would be a likely contemporary setting for such a person. Now, there are a number of popularly approved sentiments which are held to be "Truths about Life," which yet dissuade many from reaching their own inner goals. Difficulties which one encounters are not grasped as the tools they are, to strengthen and to challenge the individual. Difficulties are bemoaned by those weak in spirit as an excuse to give up. Let us list a few difficulties our hypothetical soul might encounter which could challenge his original resolve to be an ardent and effective communicator.

Financial loss is a primary stumbling block and an area where many, across all strata of your culture, find they give up their inner wisdom for the false accepted dictums. One might say the God of the Bottom Line is worshiped. In this case it is true that "God is dead," for the bottom line is not a fit goal for anyone. I am not denying the need for financial provision in order to conduct business and bring essential services and food to people. There is nothing inherently wrong with money. In fact, from our side we see its importance quite clearly. Money is a form of energy. It can be used constructively or it can be squandered.

Our person might find a first challenge or stumbling block, as he may perceive it, in the area of financial matters. Let us say that fate, in order to test his resolve, has put him in a position of holding a satisfying job at a salary he feels is inadequate for personal support. He has two options: 1) he can continue in the job, being fulfilled in his work and making necessary sacrifices in his own and perhaps his family's lifestyle, or 2) he can look for a better-paying job within or outside his own field. In order to truly test his steel, so to speak, fate would probably not allow him to easily find a higher-paying job within his field. To make more money, he would have to choose another line of work.

On the face of it, the second choice is a practical one, and one path which many people would encourage him to take, especially if he had a family to support. Few in your society would interview our fellow and focus on what was truly in his heart. They would instead stress his responsibilities as a breadwinner, and equate more bread, or possessions, with higher achievement. It becomes apparent to the reader, I'm sure, that this person's choice should have been the more difficult first path.

I should mention here that this type of decision is watched very closely from this side, and there are much spirited urgings-on toward the better decision. Our friend is not left in a vacuum but is abundantly provided with intuitive nudges toward his own greatest fulfillment. But he also receives endless dunnings, from your world, about the practical necessities of life.

When a right decision is made, there is a cheering section over here which rejoices as though our friend had just made a tie-winning touchdown. He is helped all along the way to reinforce his feeling of having made a right decision. He may be required to make many material sacrifices, yet by following his heart truly, his material needs will be met in abundance. Perhaps not the abundance defined by your society, but abundance by our more universal standards. Our friend will not want; he will have food, shelter, company and encouragement. The real key is purity of heart, being true to that inner voice.

We have strayed a bit from our purpose of illustrating life after death. But there is a method in this apparent diversion. We are attempting to show the structures which lie beneath your lives and which become clear to you upon your death. Let us proceed with our examples, then.

The financial experience is not the only typical difficulty. A person may instead have trouble succeeding in her work on the basis of her own talents. She may find that developing her skills does not come easily and that she must study hard and apply herself with great diligence in order to achieve satisfactory results. This is another obvious area of challenge. In this case, if she did not apply herself with enough energy and high standards of performance, she might be removed from her opportunity. In a typical situation, she would be fired from her job, or she might, as a business owner, be forced out of business by bankruptcy.

These are very common stumbling blocks which many people can relate to. But here is a new one for you. What about the experience of being too successful? Ironically, this is an area where people have difficulties adhering to their inner standards as well. Great financial success or personal fame can challenge individuals and dissuade them from their goals. Unfortunately, it is commonly accepted in your world that great wealth and personal renown are high marks of distinction. This is not true. The forces of success around a person are merely a test. Many times, of course, personal fame results from true achievement and the helping of others. But just as often, great wealth and influence come from financial acumen and misuse of resources, or the misapplication of resources for special interests. If a person can achieve success in his or her work and apply that success to greater good and further achievement of inner ideals, then that life is a truly accomplished one.

In sum, the newly "dead" person evaluates his own life soon upon his arrival in spirit, along such lines as we have been discussing, and he must decide whether he made the grade or not. If he did not, he undertakes some serious study in order to explore and correct the attitudes which hindered him.

There is help at every step of the way. As our traveler looks about himself, he finds a world not completely foreign to his own experience, and nothing like the religious Heaven he may have expected to find. There are no such creatures as winged angels, half human, half bird, I am afraid I must tell you, although the image makes a nice metaphor for a spirit no longer hindered by gravity or physical limitations.

As you have gathered by now, all of physical life and the spirit life as well is based upon the idea of spiritual growth, knowledge and fulfillment. Each soul yearns to know more and be more. Each step brings its own rewards and its own challenge for further growth. There is no such thing as resting on one's laurels either in this realm or yours. At every stage, another goal springs up, beckoning one onward.

And so our friend, after reviewing his life, judging his performance and assessing his failings, is drawn into further experience that will help him progress. He may find teachers and classrooms, our spirit versions, at his disposal if such is his desire. He may be led into certain affiliations with others of similar experience or complementary development, and they can be of mutual assistance. And if he has had great failings and is hindered by his own pride, he may create for himself a situation of poverty where he is trapped for a time by his own small thinking. His circumstances may seem quite distressing, and he will be unable to rise above them or improve them until his thinking changes and he is receptive to help. It seems ironic to us on this side that such souls could be too proud to desire help, for their spiritual poverty is plain to see. They elicit our great sympathy and pity, but help cannot be offered if it is not wanted.

3 | Adjusting to the New Realm

IT SHOULD be emphasized that the recently arrived traveler is not without a body. As he looks over himself, he will notice that he appears much as he did in the flesh. His body is complete, and he may even be wearing familiar clothing. There are some noticeable differences, however, from his usual physical state. His body looks similar to the way it did before, but it feels quite different.

The body is formed of a finer stuff than your earthly variety and is free from any sensations of pain, illness, discomfort, fatigue or hunger. This absolute freedom from any, however slight, feeling of malaise is exhilarating for all the new arrivals. The body is completely at ease, completely flexible, supportive, pleasurable to be attached to.

Locomotion is one of the first areas our friend is instructed in. He will find that he cannot propel himself by moving his legs as in his previous existence. He learns that his thoughts direct him wherever he wants to go. Many experience this as a pulsing motion. The entire experience in the spirit realm is perfectly and immediately responsive to thoughts. Physical life is equally responsive to thoughts, but often there is a delay in the actual physical realization.

Travel in the realms of spirit can cover great distances in an instant, actually instantaneously, or else one can move at a gradual pace through the surroundings. If a person's mind is disoriented and confused, he may find himself in the most distressing situation of flying about randomly. Of course, the body does not actually fly; it simply appears at one location, then another.

Our sense of space over here is quite different than in the physical world. For one thing, the space which various spiritual entities occupy is not necessarily attached in a logical fashion, like California and Oregon. For many, the joke "You can't get there from here" is very true in these realms. Space, in truth, is psychic, not physical. So locations may actually be overlapping, with inhabitants being unaware of their near neighbors. There are many more than three dimensions. These concepts are obviously difficult for you to absorb with your current physical orientation.

* * *

19

Our friend has witnessed his own "death"—the death of his physical body. He has been gently greeted by an old friend and shown how to move about with his newly discovered spirit body. And he has, in a flash of insight, reviewed his past life and evaluated his earthly performance. Now he is ready to get on with things, his work, his activity, and his understanding of his new home.

In order to describe what a typical newcomer perceives as he looks about himself, we must again refer to various specific case types, because there are a number of experiences, each of which is normal but which vary greatly from one to another.

Let us take the case of the person who died a natural death, say in old age, who was of good heart and generally fulfilled in her life. This person will encounter great joy upon entering these realms. We over here ardently hope that such a soul was not too indoctrinated by religious teachings to expect certain things of "heaven," for she then will find difficulties in adjusting to life here as it is. But if such a person is open-minded and capable of original perception and thought, her fondest dreams or fantasies of an afterlife will be realized, even exceeded.

She finds a world of unsurpassed beauty. There is light which suffuses every object, every corner of the realm. It's a light which comes from an interior source, an inner radiating of illumination and vitality, rather than an exterior illumination from a single source like your sun. So there are no shadows and no darkness in these regions. There are familiar objects everywhere, but they differ from those in your world in most interesting ways. Buildings, for instance, are often constructed or formed of a beautiful marble-like material, which glows with an inner luminescence and purity and is a joy to behold. There is no blowing or drifting of dirt or dust in these realms to cause buildings to deteriorate or become dirty. This applies to all objects. And while the entire physically appearing environment here is responsive to the thoughts and desires of those who dwell here, there is also a stability which is created by the more-or-less stable desires of the entire populace. Buildings, for instance, do not pop in and out of sight, but they remain until a number of spirits here decide to alter or replace them.

There is a natural countryside also, of course, because those who live here have a deep appreciation of the beauties they encountered on Earth, and so they wish to continue to enjoy them on this side. The soil is wonderfully responsive to the touch and nourishing to all kinds of plant life, yet it does not cling to the fingers or feet, nor does it dirty the homes or other areas where it is not wanted. It is a special golden color, which glimmers with a variety of other colors, and it seems magical. In fact, that is one's impression of this entire realm upon entering it. There are mystifying and luxurious colors all around. The sky shimmers like a million rainbows; bodies of water in the countryside sparkle with vitality and beauty.

You may be amused to learn that most of the inhabitants here have chosen to wear a classic uniform or dress: elegant, long, white robes which also sparkle with all the colors of the rainbow, made of a fabric with a beauty which earthly eyes have never beheld. The white robes may sound a bit unbelievable, but they are an accepted fact of life. Newcomers often wear their past earthly attire at first, but they soon discard such drab wear for the natural covering I have just described. They needn't, of course, go to any closet or cloakroom to change clothes. They need only desire to be dressed in such robes and they automatically find themselves so attired.

There are certain limitations to all the experiences here, however, and a person cannot create extravagant jewels or personal adornments at will. Jewelry is enjoyed here, but it is worn by those who have "earned" it with spiritual growth. Leaders often appear dressed in the beautiful yet simple robes, with lovely jewels, pearls or gold as adornment to their clothing or hair. Many people on Earth are enchanted with the beauties of jewelry—necklaces, rings, beaded clothing, belts, etc.—and that same appreciation and enjoyment of beauty continues here. In these realms beauty is realized to a much fuller extent, since there are no hindrances, such as the physical world supplies, to the materialization of the most lovely objects imaginable.

We have mentioned buildings, the earth-like environment, clothing and jewelry. Let me say a bit more about the "out-of-doors" setting of this spirit realm. There are idyllic countrysides, with beautiful trees, never showing a speck of disease or imperfection. All the trees grow straight and perfect, for there is no weather to bring hardship to them. Each leaf is perfect and lives without the interruption of the seasons. Much of the ground is covered with a lush grass, and this soft luxurious covering provides the walkways through the "urban" areas, around the public buildings and private homes.

Flowers of this realm bring the greatest joy and delight, to many of the new arrivals here, of all the wonders they encounter. For the flowers are of a beauty which you of the earthly realm can little even imagine. The loveliest blossoms on Earth are but a pale cousin to their counterparts in these realms. Flowers grow in every color and hue imaginable, and then beyond that there are colors that I cannot describe. Each blossom is utterly perfect, and each flower exudes a vitality and personality like you would encounter in another human being. The laws of the universe are simply more apparent in this realm than in yours.

One immutable law which you will find surprising is this: all matter has life and consciousness. Your scientists have seen this by studying atomic structures and molecular elements. But your society as a whole is utterly ignorant of this basic law. Naturally, every growing thing has life, as you know, but with a vitality far beyond what you might expect. Other forms of matter have life and consciousness also. Rocks, for example, are not the lifeless and changeless hunks that they appear to be. Rocks are living, breathing, changing portions of the universe which are endowed with a vital, if small, portion of consciousness. The same is true of all the physical objects of your world.

Here this law is visible and perceived by all. There is a "feeling" sensation one gets when confronted with any of the elements of this world. To return to our train of thought, flowers are an excellent example of this. They have a breathtaking beauty, and each petal is endowed with a pulsing life which you can feel. As you hold a flower in your hands, you can feel an energizing vitality and goodness flowing from it.

These gifts come from God and are available to the inhabitants here for their own pleasure. The God who is perceived here as the giver of all life, however, is quite different from the God defined in your churches. I will get to that distinction a bit later. The important point is that there is a loving, supportive and pervasively good aura about these spirit realms, and all who live here perceive it, are comforted by it and enjoy it immensely.

4 | Defining the Limits

IN THE above example, there is a wealth of greater detail I could give you relating to the new world beyond what I have just described, but rather than overemphasize one area, I would like to touch upon other types of experiences which are perceived by newcomers.

We defined our first traveler as an older person who died a natural death, such as from an illness.

Let's look at another type of death experience, one of violence. As we all know too well, there are many ways to die a violent death. Not all of them will bring initial difficulties for a person coming over here, but many do. As I mentioned in the introduction, since there are no such occurrences as random accidents in this universe, the victims of acts of violence have on one level elicited such acts against themselves. Sometimes it is to even up accounts from other lives, sometimes it is to stress a relationship between the person's fears and his or her reality.

Quite frequently those suffering a violent death must make exceptional mental adjustments to this life over here. They have the initial disadvantage of not having prepared themselves mentally for their own impending death. Once on this side, they have the added burden of worrying over the shocked family members they left on Earth. Victims of crime almost always have faulty notions about human behavior. Many victims of criminal acts have been perpetrators of such acts in their own lifetimes. Naturally this is true in wartime with military casualties, although I am not equating war-time combat experience with crime. But the same rules apply. It is OK to receive from others what you give out to them. This is a kind of inverse Golden Rule. We might call it the Blackened Rule.

At any rate, we have another type of violent death, and that is the apparently senseless one of a well-behaved member of society being killed by a fringe criminal element or a one-time criminal whom he may know. In most of these cases, the dead person is quite disoriented upon waking up over here. Most of them have not consciously believed in an afterlife, and in almost every case much coddling and coercion is necessary before they believe what has really happened, that they have left Earth and entered another plane of existence, equally valid and equally real.

Now, these people often must do quite a bit more soul-searching in order to evaluate their lives. Those who have been victims of criminal acts are shown that they somehow chose the role of victim and must confront their own thinking and reasoning behind such a choice.

Those who have behaved in a violent manner toward others must evaluate all their reasons for so behaving. These souls especially have many difficult lessons to learn, and they cannot escape the sins of their past. They will find much mental focusing on their former victims and their own poor thinking.

"It is most difficult for those in your world to understand this, but all events have purposes."

Then there is another kind of violent death, suicide. This involves the same kind of mental delusions as that of taking another person's life. The act of suicide can undo much good that a person has amassed through his life, and we over here always are saddened to see a person's life come to such a poor conclusion. There really are no mitigating circumstances for suicide. The greater psyche always has the individual's best interest at heart, and the conscious decision to take one's own life is contrary to these deeper intuitions. If it is best for a person to die, then the psyche or soul "arranges" for such a death to occur naturally, whether by illness or apparent accident, such as occurs so often now on your freeways. It is most difficult for those in your world to understand this, but all events have purposes, and the greater goal behind all events is human understanding and learning. Many deaths occur in a manner that will be a dramatic lesson to those remaining on Earth.

By gathering together all the deaths which we define as those occurring through violent means, I don't mean to imply all these souls are at a similar level of development. Many die during war, for instance, who are basically fulfilled people and have little difficulty adjusting over here. But a great number of such people suffer from grave misconceptions about themselves and their lives, and their experience upon passing over—to this side of the veil, so to speak—is markedly different from that described in the last chapter.

A typical person in this category will find herself in a cold, barren landscape, in contrast to the comfortable warmth of the previous illustration. There will be little of beauty or interest around her. She may find other entities who appear ugly or threatening. She indeed has taken the fears of her lifetime into the world she encounters beyond death, and it might be eons before she understands that her own mind has created these difficulties. Those who are enjoying the "higher," more pleasant realms are saddened to know of these realms of ugliness and confusion. Certain higher spirits who have been specially trained

25

may enter these realms from time to time to be available for assistance. But this assistance cannot be consummated without a certain wholesome open-mindedness on the part of the dweller as to her own need for help. Many in these realms are trapped for long periods by their own fury and confusion.

Rather than belabor the unfortunate styles of life, or death, which are experienced here, I would just like to point out an obvious conclusion. People do well to take their physical existence seriously and try to learn as much as possible during their lives. Their lessons are easier in some respects on Earth than on this side. Those who are spiritually impoverished over here have many obstacles to overcome, which are often much more difficult than when they were in the flesh. And if their sins were great, it may be a very long time before they are given a chance to atone with another life.

* * *

Now, my secretary Judy is wondering about the meaning of the title of this chapter. It refers to the very definite limitations which dwellers on this side are confronted with. Let me make an analogy. On your three-dimensional Earth, you have comparative freedom of movement. If you so desire and can find an affordable method of travel, you can journey to distant countries and visit different cultures and peoples. In our realms there are, in certain regards, greater restrictions. In a sense, you cannot travel to another country at will. It is not that there are fences or walls which prohibit movement, but there are natural laws which come into play. Like minds attract one another, and so most often people find themselves in the company of others like themselves.

Let's be specific. In some accounts of this world, numbers have been identified with various realms, and these are helpful in such discussions, or discourses, as this one. The Earth is referred to as Realm One. Actually, Realm One correlates with physical life in all its manifestations. As you might guess, there are many other planets in this universe which contain life like your own. I might as well mention this now since I won't be going into that subject in the present book.

Realm Two refers to the darker places that we have just briefly mentioned, which are created by troubled souls who are attempting to deal with their problems and confusions. If there is a corollary to the Hell mentioned in your religions it would be these regions. But there is nothing eternal about them. Always there is hope and opportunity for advancement and growth for all souls. Parenthetically, these regions are not hot but quite unpleasantly cold.

Realm Three is the first of the spirit realms of light and beauty, and most of you in your world will come to this area after death. This is the world of joy, meaning and beauty that we described in the last chapter. All in all, there are seven realms, with the highest being that of God, or All-That-Is.

My point in numbering and naming these realms is to clarify that travel between realms is not automatic. In order to explore a higher realm, one must obtain training and a guide to lead the way. All souls can go to a "lower" realm at will [except from Realm Two to the physical world, Realm One]. Individuals have the strength to rise above a lower realm as they please, although visitors going from Realm Three to Two often must also be accompanied by a guide who helps them stay protected from degrading elements or unhappy experiences.

These, briefly, are the limits of the universe. They are formed from within each soul and they define the growth which has occurred and which ought to be undertaken. There are limitations in spirit just as in the flesh, and these limitations are good; they help each entity to seek and find the best path.

27

5 | The Life of the Spirit

DEATH is not the barren cessation of consciousness that most imagine. Neither is it a linking-up with God or some other entity so that one's own personality is lost. Death in many ways is more lively than the Earth lives you all know. Your consciousness literally expands, becoming more "you." Experiencing this continuation of consciousness beyond the physical body brings a special sense of exhilaration and exuberance. In addition, a feeling of consummate safety pervades these realms; everyone here realizes that nothing can be destroyed.

In your world there is much concern over the nuclear arms race. It is appropriate that there should be an outcry to halt this development, for it threatens your world. But I would also like to add a few thoughts on this subject. Humankind is not God. Humanity cannot create the Earth and cannot destroy it. It is true the power of the atom is mighty. But the power of consciousness is the mightiest of all. There is a God who watches over your world. I am one of the sub-gods who watch over you. I reside in Realm Six, while All-That-Is (or God) resides in

Realm Seven. I am in contact with this highest realm. Though I do not understand this vast realm completely, I understand much. And I have several messages to relay which should be of comfort to all of you.

No life can be destroyed. God (Her)Himself could not destroy a life, even if (S)He wanted; the immutable laws of the universe are based on the vast power of consciousness.

Consciousness is eternal. Therefore the life of the mind and heart are eternal. If a nuclear bomb should destroy your world, so that living creatures could no longer survive on its face, then you spirits who require physical expression for your growth would be given a new world. There are many planets besides your own, and vast numbers, millions of them, already support life much like your own. There have been worlds destroyed by humans in much the same manner that you now fear threatens your own world.

So take heart. It is good for you all, as individuals, to fight against the insanities of your times. But do not despair. People do not have the power to destroy the human race. The human race has a most secure place in the universe. It is here to stay.

* * *

Let's talk some more about the new environments people enter on this side of the veil.

In discussing Realms Two and Three, I do not wish to make it sound as though things are black and white over here: that people are good or evil and therefore go to Realm Three or Two, depending. As you know, things are not black and white in life, nor are they in spirit. No person is completely good and no one completely bad; there is a bit of each in all people. Generally it is known that a person's life has a certain timbre, a certain over-all quality which is a distinguishing feature.

If, in an overall sense, people have shown understanding and compassion for their neighbors and have sought to help them, then they will reap the rewards of good life over here.

On the other hand, if people were preoccupied with their own status or material gain, so that they were blind to the needs and desires of those around them, then they have some learning to do before entering a realm of light and beauty. Perhaps they really have a good heart after all and see the error of their earthly attitudes quite readily. They may progress very rapidly over here, much to the pleasure of all who know them.

However, and here is one of the distinctions between gray and black, if the life's errors were very deep, if not only selfishness and uncaring attitudes prevailed, but if people also went out of their way to cause pain to others, then the path over here will be long and difficult.

I don't enjoy going into grisly details about such matters, because they are most unpleasant to me, to my secretary here who must read them and then type them, and to my readers, whom I know to be of finer sensibilities. But I do want people of your Earth to understand something important about universal law. In mentioning these things I am not trying to strike fear in the hearts of my readers, threatening them so they will be good. I am stating a universal law as a gentle warning to those who have troubled spirits and confused minds. No evil action can be easily forgotten. There is true justice in the universe, and this justice is meted out from within each consciousness. There is no cosmic police force. No enlightened soul here would have the heart for such a task. All in my realm desire to help others, to do good, to create beauty and to have fun.

There is true justice in the universe, but it is meted out from within each consciousness. There is no cosmic police force.

There is abundant help offered to troubled souls. But their own punishments come from within. Now, I want to say something else. There are no men, not one, who are truly evil in their hearts. All men and women yearn to be good, to become good, to grow and expand.

There are, obviously, many people who do apparent evil and bring harm to others. This is caused by their own confused thinking. They literally do not know what they are doing. In most cases these deluded minds are attempting to correct what they perceive to be an imbalance. They are utterly ignorant of the truth of their lives and this world. They are to be pitied, not hated or cursed. They will force themselves to struggle painfully through all the evil experiences they have caused others.

These deluded spirits create worlds of ugliness and pain for themselves, worlds where only they themselves reside. In the world of spirit, the more enlightened souls never come in contact with these troubled ones unless they desire to offer assistance or insight.

These unhappy corners of the universe are as varied in their manifestations as are the confused thoughts of their inhabitants. But there are several typical environments found in Realm Two. The simplest and least-repugnant is that of a house which appears like an unclean hovel. A number from your society who were, say, more interested in amassing wealth and prestige for themselves than in opening their hearts to others, find themselves in such an environment. To their own perception, they are quite alone. They have in their lifetimes closed their hearts to all others, so in this realm they reap the harvest of this thinking. They remain alone until they open their minds to the subject of their own poor thinking; once they are open for help, they often can progress quite rapidly.

In the unusual case of a person who has caused much pain to others, say a man who has killed others in a vicious, cruel manner while on Earth, this man is almost inhuman in his heart. He has had none of the finer qualities of human spirit, and he too will find in this afterlife that he reaps what he has sown.

31

In the afterlife, a vicious person might appear like a reptile or an ugly beast.

He may find himself without a human-like form; he might appear like a reptile or an ugly beast of some sort, crawling through cold, tangled swamps, never finding comfort or pleasure. If this sounds like a hell or a purgatory to you, I guess you would be right. The important point, however, is that this man, through the meanness of his earthly motives and actions, has created his own reality on this side. He may crawl on his belly for eons before standing on two feet again, before he is ready to try once more to be human. And then he will earn for himself another chance and a means for atoning for his sins against others in the past.

Growth is assured. Because consciousness is eternal, each single fragment of consciousness will eventually know itself, know truth, and travel in the realms of light. This is my message to you all: there is stability in the universe, a great abiding good which pervades it, and hope and joy available to all creatures, to every speck of life and consciousness which travels among the stars.

Now, we have covered what we all consider to be the worst part, the bad news, when people are misguided, confused and when their lives have shut out the natural urgings of the heart, those impulses to be kind and helpful to those around one. In this case, folks have troubles over here. I believe we have said enough to convey the kind of difficulties encountered by such people. Let's turn now to the realms of light and their inhabitants.

* * *

Invariably upon death, people of good heart will find themselves in what I have referred to as Realm Three. In some cases, they have in their past inhabited one of the higher realms, but because of the narrowing of memory necessary for physical life, these people will need to broaden their minds and "remember" quite a few things before going on.

I have mentioned to Judy that she herself normally resides in Realm Four. She is now embarrassed by this disclosure and worried that by so naming levels of spiritual achievement, people might develop competitive spirit. It might not be such a bad thing for people on Earth to strive for spiritual advancement, knowing that such a thing is represented by an overflowing of love and understanding for others, not necessarily overt acts of charity or churchgoing. In fact, Ms. Laddon feels extremely humble about herself, an attitude which is quite appropriate. People should not feel superior to one another by any standards, whether they be job status, material wealth, educational background, race, religion, or even spiritual attainment. It is important to recognize that each man, woman and child is unique, that each person has inner goals which he or she is addressing in any one life, and that these goals and the methods and attitudes which will lead to their fulfillment might vary greatly from the next person. "Love thy neighbor" is beautiful advice. Yet all people need to respect themselves and their own identity first of all. Then they can find magnanimity in their hearts for others.

Just a few more words about these various realms. In private sessions, I have revealed to Judy that a small percentage of people have chosen to come to Earth who normally reside in Realm Four. Ms. Laddon herself is one. She does not consciously have any recollection, naturally, of this background, but I can see it clearly. There is also a very small percentage of your total Earth population that comes from Realm Five. It is hard to define the realities of these realms, but enough to say that each level represents the attainment of a larger consciousness — consciousness literally expands by joining up with others' consciousness. With that enlargement comes a greater understanding of truths.

To put these things in perspective, let me say this: The man you know as Jesus Christ, and certain other historical figures whom I won't now name, came from a system outside the normal Earth-centered consciousness altogether. Christ, historically, resided in Realm Six and still does today. His consciousness was so great that he couldn't be compared to a normal man. This larger consciousness was able to tap powers which are not normally available to humans. These powers, by which those in his world were able to witness miracles, enabled the people of his time to believe in him and give credence to his teachings.

I don't want to dwell on this subject very much. My secretary and I both have a distaste for religious fanaticism or religiosity in many forms. It is sad to see the confused dogma which has, over the centuries, come to be accepted along with the truthful teachings of Christianity and other religions. Too, we aren't trying to start a religious movement here.

Let me say this: there is truth in all the world's religions. But none of them is clearly more truthful than the others. What I am trying to accomplish by speaking to your world I do completely outside of a religious framework. We are interested in reaching individuals and telling them to listen to the inner voice. Truth is within your own heart. Your deepest intuitions will bring you the greatest truth you can know in physical life. This touching of deeper truths is accessible to every person. Each human being has a soul, and this soul carries the wisdom of the universe. Just listen; that's all that needs to be done. But that in itself requires a certain discipline and understanding. You must first acknowledge that there is truth in your own heart. And then you must make the effort to clear away the clutter of normal thoughts, those compelling, endless images and long speeches about the pressing day-to-day concerns. Try to pause from these thoughts and listen to your heart truly. You will always be answered.

* * *

My intention in this chapter is to come back to a description of Realm Three, the new country or landscape where most of you will find yourselves at death. We have had an interesting glimpse of it in our first chapters, and now I'd like to flesh it out in greater detail.

The physical surroundings are utterly breathtaking, so far do they surpass any beauties you have enjoyed on Earth. Yet they do not overwhelm the senses; they appear to each viewer to be completely harmonious and lovely to the eye. Though the perception of color and texture is much wider here than on Earth, yet nothing seems garish or unattractive. Every single soul who comes to this realm is awestruck by its utter beauty, harmony and sense of emotional wholeness. It is as though any negative elements which are encountered on Earth have been completely eliminated, and the beauties and joys of the Earth plane have been multiplied a hundredfold.

Yet there is no state of utter bliss for the inhabitants here. This is an important point to interject. After you die, you still feel like yourself. There are merely a number of greater truths which you now understand. Sometimes these truths cause people here to feel quite a bit of remorse and regret.

We have admitted that life situations are not black and white, and so many people who have earned a right to reside in this lovely realm also fully realize the mistakes they made while on Earth. If their mistaken attitudes caused pain to others on Earth, then they feel all the more regret.

Let me give an example. Let's say a person lived a full life and was very loving to her family and close circle of friends. But let us also say that this same person, who is basically good and kind, had accepted a vein of thinking by which she felt superior to another race on Earth, or people of other countries, or educational levels, etc. This person may have been cold and uncaring in her attitudes toward a whole segment of the Earth's inhabitants. When, over here, her mind has expanded to see the folly of such bigotry, then she will undoubtedly feel remorse and look for ways to correct past wrongs. There are many opportunities for satisfying her desires. There are many occupations over here which she can undertake to provide this function. Plus, a time will come when this person may decide to be reborn on Earth with hopes for overcoming these errors of the past.

We'll now touch on some occupations which are carried on in this world. I'm sure the term occupation will seem out of place in a discussion of a so-called spirit world, since so many on your plane have accepted the religious description of Heaven as a land of leisure and exalted appreciation of music. In part, this description is touching to me, since it is a metaphor for the pure nature of music and its emotional validity as a means of expressing great joy. There certainly is beautiful music over here, with such a breadth of impact, both sensory and emotional, that it is hard to describe with words. But in the same way as many in your world are not very interested in music, so many here do not address themselves often to musical interests. As a general rule, those passionate interests which you have had in life continue to be expressed and explored in this realm. The opportunities for learning over here are far greater than you know.

Naturally there are many occupations undertaken on Earth which have no parallel here. In fact, the list is a mile long. Just think of it: any occupation which has to do with sustaining physical life and interacting with the physical realm is either drastically altered over here or not applicable at all. Spirit bodies do not require food, so strike out myriad Earth-type jobs, from farming to grocery stores, cooking to restaurants. However, gardening is passionately pursued over here, and there are fruit-bearing trees whose produce is greatly enjoyed. A note for those overly fond of the table: at all levels of existence, people create their own circumstances to a large degree. If one craves earthly-type food, one may continue to enjoy it over here until the craving is assuaged and those energies are directed elsewhere.

The occupations of this realm are as varied as those you are familiar with on Earth—even more so since there are new potentials for activity not possible or dreamed of in your realm.

It is true many Earth occupations are not needed here, such as everything dealing with physical materials and other unnecessary commodities, like money.   Eliminate bankers, investment analysts, the list goes on and on.   However, I will name a few occupations which are undertaken with relish here, and which take on new meaning given the wider freedoms.   All variety of the arts are enjoyed wholeheartedly.   Music, especially, is a joy to all. Composers allow their creativity free reign, without the limitations encountered in earthly life of time constraints and gradual physical deterioration.   Many of your former well-known composers have continued their work over here, producing many more masterpieces than they were able to on Earth.   Then, too, musicians and vocalists have broader opportunities here,   with the instruments available and the expressions of the spiritual voice.

Art, music, social work, teaching, all are popular occupations on the other side.

What else?   Teaching is an activity integral to all walks of existence.   Learning on many levels and toward many different goals is most accessible and even encouraged.   It is utterly voluntary, of course, so all students and teachers alike enjoy these activities immensely.   As you might imagine, many study the Earth, its true history—quite different from your textbooks—its promise, methods of interaction from our realm to yours, and countless other areas.

Social work, as you think of it, is a popular interest.   There are many people who come here confused, spiritually and "physically" weak, even in their spirit bodies, due to difficult, long illnesses prior to death or lengthy periods of psychological malaise.

They are met by loving spirits, old and new friends alike, who are eager to help them adjust and become strong. Just as on the Earth plane, there are many souls here who derive the greatest pleasure from helping others.

As you may be guessing by now, an individual entering Realm Three often continues to have the same interests which he or she had in physical life and is delighted to find an environment of unparalleled, rich opportunities for indulging those interests. If one has lived a life working hard at an occupation which was not enjoyable, here such a pattern is joyfully reversed as one's deepest desires are realized.

6 Going to Work in Realm Three

I BELIEVE we should have an entire chapter devoted to this subject, since it will be of intense interest to many of our readers.

There are numerous misconceptions about our world. Many people blithely accept the false notion that consciousness ends at death. Hence you hear the disgruntled comment from those who are dissatisfied with their earthly life or health: "Yes, but it's better than the alternative." Many souls on this side chuckle over the spiritual naivete´ of that notion.

Then, too, for those religious persons who contemplate a Heaven over here, many are only vaguely expecting a world of any interest to them at all. The idea of saintly spirits wandering around singing and playing harps is understandably not very enticing. The idea itself is disconcerting. Trying to envision their continued existence after death, people wonder if any aspects of their normal, familiar personalities will remain. Do they need to force themselves to enjoy singing and harp music if they never have enjoyed such activites before? Must they give up all their earthly interests and passions? Will all the really fun activities of their lives be utterly lost, forever?

Naturally there is great amazement among such people when they actually arrive over here. It is a kind of Heaven, filled with unutterable joys; yet they remain themselves—not perfect, celestial beings. Earthly interests often can be indulged over here with such concentration and satisfying results as never could have been imagined.

Further examples of occupations are meant to relate to interests in your society. Judy wonders about occupations taken up by people from more primitive societies, who might have been mostly occupied in life with finding food and creating shelter. As an aside from our main topic, let me remind readers that such primitive people often have indulged, while on Earth, their own passionate interests in the arts—painting, basket and pottery making, songwriting and performing, and storytelling. They continue such activities over here. In fact, they interact quite beautifully with those who arrive from more "advanced" cultures. There is a wonderfully complementary aspect to this interaction. In your society the logical portion of the human mind has been developed, or should I say overdeveloped. In their societies the intuitive portion of the mind has been allowed to flower. Each can learn from the other many lessons. So there is much interaction and "spirited" communication of many peoples in these realms!

Remember that the basic soul, the heart of every personality, is without race or nationality or any other artificial division. The brotherhood of man is not an empty phrase; it carries the weight of universal truth.

"The brotherhood of man is not an empty phrase."

What might you expect to do after you die? We assume you had your basic orientation here, and perhaps a lengthy vacation enjoying the sights. After a time, however, you become somewhat uneasy, wanting to be mentally occupied by some fruitful activity. Let's say you were an architect or contractor on Earth and are fascinated by the buildings of this realm. Is there any work for you here?

There is, indeed. But before you can express your natural abilities, you must undergo extensive training. The construction of buildings in these places is very different from those you have experienced on Earth. There are no tools of the trade, for instance: no shovels, no tractors, no hammers, nails. No wooden boards, no concrete, no trucks, tresses, steel girders, cranes. All activities here are essentially mental. Even the construction of our "physical" edifices is based on mental activity; but it is not accomplished without training, knowledge, study, design and, in the end, mental work.

Let us look at the process. The first item to be attended to is the purpose of the building. It has been determined by many that a new edifice is needed for some reason. Counselors from a "higher" realm have been consulted and are in agreement. The architects and planners have been made aware of the group desire for a new building, and they begin to work on plans. Without actual paper, pencils, drafting tables and T-squares, they come up with a plan that is approved. Then, without so much as a scrap of wood or a hammer, the architects and planners gather, empty-handed, at the building site. Through mental concentration they build a thought-form which embodies the design elements they have already determined. This thought-form looks like a misty, hazy building, not quite solid, but visible enough to be studied. They wander all around this thought-form, studying, analyzing, comparing it to the needs and purposes intended. They make adjustments where necessary. Then the form gains substance and solidity. When all are convinced that the final form is perfect, they mentally call to the higher spirits for a breath of life. This could be compared metaphorically with Michelangelo's famous painting of God bestowing life with a tip of His finger to the awaiting man. The form has been created and perfected, but it can only be truly realized with the force of life.

All who live in these realms are intimately familiar with the flowing of this life-giving energy. It is apparent all around. To describe it to those of you focused on earthly reality is difficult. But knowing your desire to understand, plus, I hope, your open-mindedness, I will attempt to describe this as clearly as I can.

The building, in effect, comes alive. By that I do not mean it throbs and pulses and dances a jig around the square. But the shadowy outlines fill in; it takes on solid shape and substance. The haziness of its first, tentative form disappears, and a beauty and lustre and vibrancy coalesce to form the final structure. The job is completed, and the edifice is here to stay. There is far greater permanency here than you would expect, for time does not alter its beauty nor its integrity. Only when it is desired that the structure be altered will such happen.

You can imagine the enjoyment which the architects feel in this process. All the drudgery related to their earthly labor is gone up here: no administrative duties, no offices and telephones to arrange for, no pencils and paper to supply, nor endless working drawings and artists' renderings to laboriously create. Only the most pure forms of creativity and talent are needed for this work. The rewards, a stunning final product not hampered by budget restraints, building codes, material or weather limitations, bring tremendous satisfactions.

Flowers grow not from seeds planted in soil but from a seed of thought.

There are many other jobs here with gratifications just as substantial as those for architects. A prime example is gardening and horticulture. Naturally this field varies greatly from what you know on Earth, but the satisfactions are increased a hundredfold. Let me describe the growing of a single flower. This is not accomplished from seeds planted in the soil. This occurs from a seed of thought. Those who desire to delve into gardening undergo an apprenticeship which prepares them for dealing with the mysterious ways of our spirit realm.

First, the gardener and students study the blueprints, so to speak, of various flowers. Varieties are far more numerous than you would guess. After much study, they focus their attention on an empty pot of soil. They gradually form an image of the flower in their mind, and mentally sculpt that shape in the space above the flower pot. Just as the architects' structure appeared shadowy at first, so does this first tentative flower. It is a thought-form. They examine it from every angle to determine if it is perfect. Sometimes there are flaws, and these are corrected. Sometimes the "creative gardeners" scrap the first effort and start all over again. But when they have determined the flower is perfect, they allow it to take on solidity, a full, colorful shape of substance. Apparently, the flower is then perfect and complete. But not so. At this stage it still lacks life. So with their thoughts, the gardeners call to the higher realms for the life force, and such is immediately granted. The flower pulses with life. It exudes a vibrating, good and replenishing force; plus it is blessed with heavenly fragrance.

Flowers here all differ in that they never wilt or die. They exist as long as it is desired that they should do so. There are also garden designers, or landscape architects, who arrange flowers, shrubbery and trees in enchanting gardens around the public places and private homes. Just as on Earth, there are many here who enjoy gardening as a delightful hobby, complementing their other work. There are always many people ready to help you learn the ropes, so to speak, and aid in laying out your own private garden.

One last note about the nature of flowers. Many Earth varieties have a number of buds on a single stem, which open up one at a time. In these realms all the blossoms on a single stem are open at the same time. This everlasting nature has the effect of pleasing everyone here, and it is one of the visual metaphors for life in these realms. Spirit forms do not age, deteriorate or die. They go on and on, according to their own season. For a person, growth and vitality increase one's power as new lessons are learned, new connections made. The joy of this process is felt and appreciated by all.

Such, then, is the joy of gardening here. Flowers are created, not by "nature," but by the ordinary inhabitants who understand that life force comes from the power of thoughts and consciousness. The actual life force, granted from "above," is always immediately available, never denied.

Another occupation interacts with a type of computer. These computers are like a source bank or collection of thought records which form natural organizations, and which are conveniently referred to by those who desire such information. They are also called archives. We have a very powerful "library" system here, and this is a part of it. The form this information takes depends upon the desired use of it. There are many volumes of books here, but people also have access to specific "printouts" of information they desire about one particular thing. Unlike on Earth, there is no hardware to speak of, for such a mechanical tool is not necessary. All that is needed is the desire for knowledge; it then becomes available.

Many enjoy perusing our library of Earth history. These books are fascinating compared to their Earth counterparts, because they contain the entire truth surrounding historic events. They not only tell what occurred in history as you think of it, but they reveal the complete sequence of events, embellished with all the deepest motives of the people involved. This is powerfully different from the history in your schools and universities, and it holds many lessons about human nature.

Cosmic microfilm contains the truth behind all of human history, including the hidden motives and thoughts of all people involved.

There are also voluminous records available regarding all souls in the universe. These are sometimes called the Akashic records. They are not physically materialized, naturally, although they are available on a kind of cosmic microfilm, a record created by thought patterns that is retained by the universe. These records are made available by those who have chosen such work—spiritual library science professionals, you might say. There are certain understandings necessary and a certain training prerequisite to being able to locate this information. In their work, then, these professionals aid others in their searches and in their study.

A certain amount of record-keeping is involved in the birth and death processes of your world. Too, many newcomers over here wonder of the whereabouts of their friends. They must seek aid to discover whether these friends have returned to the flesh, traveled to other spirit regions or are nearby and available for interaction. This record-keeping is not cold and impersonal but undertaken with the greatest sense of warmth and personal fulfillment. People here are never just a number, for they automatically sense the fullness of all the other personalities here, and there is a vivid sense of friendship and camaraderie which pervades the whole environment.

There are many other occupations. The arts, for instance, are thoroughly enjoyed here but without the artifice and materialistic motives which sometimes accompany your contemporary artists' endeavors. Then, too, there are delightful museums of these artworks, plus all the originals of great works of art from the Earth plane. These originals make their physical counterparts on Earth look pale by comparison, because they embody the artists' true intentions without the actual obstacles which compromise quality in order to emerge in physical form. These museums are entertaining and also illuminating about the artists' motives and impulses in their art.

We have mentioned musical composition. Added to that is the occupation of instrument-maker. Musical instruments are created as all other things here are created, with the mind. The variety here is far wider than you could imagine. Sounds produced during performances in this realm are too heavenly to describe with words, but I will say this: a much larger percentage of the populace here appears at concerts. There is another indescribable feature of these concerts unique to this side of the veil. This music creates visual forms, beautiful pulsing forms of brilliant colors which rise in crescendos as a concert takes place. So the listeners, and viewers, of these occasions are utterly enthralled by the experience. It is multisensual. At the beginning of a performance, the color form takes on tentative shape which gains strength as the concert progresses. It changes subtly throughout the concert, and when the music is over, it lingers for some time, reminiscent of the event which recently took place. The delight and spontaneity of the "music of the spheres" or heavenly music is quite different, I'm sure, from what most of you would have imagined!

To proceed with our example, the nursing and medical professions are fairly well represented here, but with remarkable differences from your side. The spirit body is made of a much finer stuff than the physical flesh, but it still has a material manifestation. It is self-healing and, from moment to moment, even self-created. That is, personalities who advance to the higher realms eventually discard these "astral" bodies completely, no longer needing to clothe their consciousnesses within such forms. But those in Realm Three, and even Realms Four and Five, find it comforting and convenient to wear the familiar body.

The arrival of newcomers presents certain health problems which require tactful "medical" treatment. Most often, this is

45

simply the gentle teaching and instruction by "nurses" of the nature of this realm. Many who first wake up over here have so closely identified themselves with physical disabilities, illnesses, pain and weakness that they create correllating maladies in their spirit bodies. They are gently taught about this realm and are given assistance in becoming whole and full of strength.

Aging also fits into this category. I should point out that each of you who holds this book in your hands has an "astral" body within your physical one. It is this body which leaves you when you are dreaming or when "out-of-body" excursions take place. This body cannot be seen by your earthly eyes as a rule, but it does exist and it even has weight, a couple of ounces on average. As the human body ages, the astral body too takes on identical characteristics. Sometimes there are exceptions to this, such as in dismemberment; occasionally the person continues to "feel" the missing limb since the astral body is yet intact.

When people die of old age, they often find themselves in their old, familiar images when they first arrive here. In time they will learn to manipulate themselves and regain the full vigor of their prime years. By the same token, those who die as infants or children also soon reach their prime of life and so remain as long as they wish. Many, naturally, return to the Earth plane eventually and take on new identities.

7 The Role of Science

I'M DEVOTING a new chapter to this single occupation because it is such an important one in your world. Science is the new religion of the developed countries in the 20th century, you might say. Yet many are now asking, "What good has our science done for us? The culmination of our discoveries has resulted in the bomb, which now poses a greater threat to the human race than ever before encountered."

What I wish to say is this: in the "developed" nations, your race as a whole has decided to pursue the course of the logical mind. This has been allowed to happen with friendly encouragement from this side. It is important to understand that for every event in your physical world, there have been psychic constructs supporting such an event from our invisible realm. I have stated before that there are no accidents in the universe. The development of your sciences certainly falls into this category. There are purposes to these sciences which will help people learn certain lessons not possible by taking other routes. Let me restate this. We have pointed out the development of intuitive portions of the mind in primitive societies. In your culture these intuitive portions have been sublimated in favor of enhancing and developing the logical-thinking processes. Your sciences illustrate this course.

But scientists are not without intuitions also, although they may not acknowledge them per se. I can say without exception that all the scientific advancements of your age have occurred with the consent and assistance of spirits from our realm. This does not mean to detract from the fine accomplishments of your earthly scientists. I am merely stressing, with an example which further advances our basic point, that all activities of your realm are supported from this side.

How does this happen? The answer is that there are many scientists in our midst who also study, research, form theories and experiment to discover truths about the universe. As you might imagine, their options are somewhat broader than those of Earth scientists. We have several branches of scientific research over here. Some are studying our world, the entire universe as we perceive it, and others are more specialized. Many scientists narrow their studies to the Earth and technological advances which could help the Earth populations. When they have perfected their findings and they deem it appropriate to share these with Earth scientists, then a certain procedure is begun.

First, the scientist discusses his or her ideas and findings with counselors and higher authorities on this side. If it is agreed that the Earth inhabitants are ready for such information, then it is made possible for the spirit scientist to convey his/her findings to the Earth scientist. This is done through several channels. During the dream state much scientific information is introduced. This can then be absorbed by a portion of the brain and later made available to the individual by a flash of "insight." Too, thoughts are sometimes directly urged on the individual. An Earth scientist may simply, out of the blue, be struck by an urge or thought to try a new approach in solving a problem, or to redefine and start off in an altogether new direction. Those scientists who allow their intuitions the freest reign will be the most advanced.

The sharing of scientific secrets or information from this realm to yours does not mean this information will always be used for the greater good of humankind. But please understand this: advancements are given in the hopes that they will be applied to good ends in helping people. We all understand that humans are free to make mistakes and misappropriate power to improper ends, and this freedom is essential to their being. Therefore, we do not withhold experience simply because it might be misused.

"Why, though," many of you might ask, "was nuclear technology given to us? The first thing we did with it was create a horrendous war machine." To that question I answer: It was not fated nor predetermined that people would create nuclear holocaust with this technology. In fact it was ardently hoped that this would not happen, that the power of the atom would be used for peaceful purposes. Such is its potential.

We all knew that man in his development was ready to handle such a powerful technology but that it would tax his spiritual fortitude to the greatest extent. And so it has. Reflect a moment. A thousand years or two thousand years ago, nuclear technology was not introduced on Earth because people were not ready for it. The weapons would have been used immediately and would have destroyed the Earth. Your Earth has not yet been destroyed by madmen in control of nuclear weapons. You may be close to it, we note. But this can be considered a marvelous spiritual challenge to your time. You have to get spiritually smart, fast! Nuclear weapons will force this growth upon you. They can be a wonderful aid, if you think about it.

Prior to this technology and many of the scientific advancements of this century, the inhabitants of the Earth allowed themselves to feel insulated from one another. This smallness of mind is not possible in your age when you realize that the Earth is a small place. You are all tied together inextricably. Humankind must behave as if the welfare of one nation depended upon the health and welfare of all others.

The existence of nuclear weapons, and the possibility of nuclear holocaust, might force the development of a world peace organization and a legitimate world government. Despite all the terrible conflicts of the past, war is not inevitable. It accomplishes nothing of lasting value. War in your time could, indeed, destroy the Earth that supports you.

We have the most ardent hopes that this will not come to pass. But to be perfectly honest, one of the reasons I come at this time to speak to you is to help encourage clear thinking during this critical period of your Earth's history.

From my realm, we create worlds. I see millions of planets with human life on them. We never become calloused to these worlds simply because the universe is immense. Every portion of it is precious. Your life, the life of each individual, is precious to us and of great concern. You would be touched, as individuals, to realize the many souls on this side who are interested in your welfare, and who help you and urge you to your greatest life accomplishment. There is much lively interaction over here to determine what are the best methods by which to help you.

In a later chapter I will discuss the souls who are "assigned" to you and whose own fulfillment is interrelated with your own.

You are never alone. Please be comforted in that knowledge.
Your innermost thoughts are known to us, and your deepest desires, too. Yet you are not in any sense controlled by spirits over
here. You each are your own person. I want you to know that
truth and wisdom are always available to you; the channel is
through your own heart, your own intuitions. If you follow the
urgings of your heart, then you will surely find the path to your
own best realization and growth.

**Your life, the life of each individual,
is precious to us and of great concern.
You would be touched, as individuals,
to realize the many souls on this side
who are interested in your welfare,
and who help you and urge you to your
greatest life accomplishment.**

8 Journey beyond Realm Three

WE HAVE now discussed in some detail the shape and life of
Realm Three, the world where people find themselves after shed-
ding their physical bodies. Yet far from being disembodied,
these souls have a body just as attuned to its surroundings as you
do. In fact, the residents of this realm would testify that they
feel more alive than they ever did on Earth. This is because the
sense of understanding is greater. Each individual's world has
been enlarged.

Now, some of you will not be satisfied by just this description alone. Although once you are in Realm Three, you may have to be satisfied, since you will stay there, almost exclusively, until you are reborn. It is not a restrictive world. It is large, beautiful, expansive. Too, each soul who so desires is given glimpses of worlds beyond.

In the same context, I wish to give you a glimpse of the worlds beyond Realm Three. It cannot be more than just a glimpse, however, because your minds could not fully grasp what I will attempt to describe.

I have asked much of you already, I know, to try to imagine the personality surviving the physical body. Most of you identify yourselves so intimately with your bodies that you cannot imagine one without the other. But here, of course, we know the eternal nature of spirit and the purely temporal nature of the physical form.

As we have shown, in Realm Three life goes on in a similar vein as it did on Earth. Naturally, the changes from Earth life are dramatic, but the similarities are, too. Most souls identify themselves with their own body, even though they now understand they can alter their bodies to their own desires. Their world is an apparently physical one, surrounded by breathtakingly beautiful objects, a natural landscape, buildings, and so on. Yet the emotional tone of the realm is clear to everyone—it relates to the importance of helping others and taking joy in existence. The sense of a loving God, a "holy spirit," so to speak, pervades everywhere.

As souls progress spiritually, they advance beyond this level. There are certain first signs, or steps, to this growth. A growing disinterest in the apparently material world around them is one indication of the ability to go further. Then, too, there is an increasing joyfulness in the heart, a feeling that one will burst with the happiness which is felt here and in one's love for others.

A part of the growth pattern in these spirit realms is a difficult one to explain; it is a joining together of consciousness. I could liken it to a sexual experience that you on Earth enjoy. There is still sexual pleasure in these realms, by the way, but quite different—more fun—than you experience! I will drop this parenthetical note, even though I have sparked some interest, I'm sure, and I will mention sex more fully later on. But this joining together of consciousness is like sex, as I said, in that it connects two beings who are already intimately joined in love and understanding. On Earth a greater joy is experienced in bodily union; the pinnacle of this experience, the orgasm, is an ecstasy of pleasure and fulfillment. Without drawing this parallel too closely, let me say that the joining of consciousnesses intimately gives an even greater sense of ecstasy; a greater knowing is possible, plus an abiding love is consummated. It is a marriage of mind, of spirit, of impetus, interests and goals. It is satisfying to greater depths of emotion than you can experience or than you can recall.

This is the joy of growth. Each of you, growing up from childhood, experience tremendous growth, each level unfolding like a flower, leaving you grateful for the enlarged understanding. Spiritual growth continues here. The pace is even greater than an adult on Earth has experienced since infancy.

So then, to summarize this interesting message to you, which is really quite esoteric stuff: the spirit has joined up with other consciousnesses in order to grow, and thereby progresses to new spiritual realms. This joining has several attributes. First of all, the individual parts which have joined still remain aware of their individuality. That essence is never destroyed. But now there is an intimate sense of a larger wholeness. The parts are familiar with every other part of the whole. This is very interesting and creates a new world of experience, a gestalt of experience. You could liken it to Earth experience in this way: imagine that your mind, now focused on yourself alone, were also completely aware of the lives of another two people. Let's say you were three people at once, aware of yourself as an individual, yet also aware of two other people, whom you deeply love and admire. You would now understand their reality as experienced in their own minds.

This is an apt analogy. This experience of joining up consciousnesses carries a great vitality to it. It expands one's understanding of others immeasurably. It increases one's perception of mental events, mental things to do. All of a sudden, there are three movies, figuratively speaking, which are being shown simultaneously, and you are aware of them all, even though you may be watching one more closely than the others.

So, one still knows one's own individuality. That is protected for eternity, and is sacred. One also is stimulated by this joining of consciousness, and this in itself opens up new worlds. Now, your activities and desires have expanded greatly, as have the capacities to perform them. Many entities dwell for long periods, ages, on the interesting new activities which are available. Yet above all else is the same desire and yearning to be of help to other souls, to teach those who do not yet understand the greater truths of the universe. The larger beings or gestalts have greater ability to so teach, for they can take many forms and are intuitively more nimble in responding to a student's need.

The physical form now is a convenience to be used on occasion but also can be discarded at will. The consciousness, the personality or entity or whatever you wish to call this very real and vital soul, no longer needs a single body or image for its own identity. In fact, a body is too restrictive for this large intelligence. There is what you might call a "personality essence" which abides without form but is an intensity of thought, perception, experience and understanding. It is able to take on many forms at once, or none at all. Travel, where necessary, is instantaneous. Identification of like entities is instantaneous. Understanding and rapport with one's colleagues is also accomplished with ease, joy and much good humor, all without the convenience of a physical image or body at all.

53

Love is not a cliche but the truest aspect of this universe.

You can see the difficulties I encounter in trying to convey this reality. It is most strange to relate to an Earth-consciousness. My main objective in covering this ground with you is to indicate the variety and breadth of experience and understanding which lie before you. There is no need, now or ever, to be bored with existence or to feel trapped by it. You are meant to spread your wings and fly, in concert with your friends, through this great universe. Please know that there is a God, and many lesser gods or "angels," who love you dearly and will help you learn about this flight. We, too, want this growth for you, and we cherish you. More than anything else, it is your love for others that will urge you onward in your goals, your love for others that will bring you your greatest joy and deepest, most enriching experience.

Love is not an empty phrase. It is not a cliche. It is the truest aspect of this universe that I can describe. For it conveys the interaction and vitality of all souls with one another, and it carries within it the proverbial power and the glory. It cannot be faked, nor does it need to be. All people feel love for some aspect of life and for some of their fellows. As you open your heart to your deepest intuitions, this love for others will expand. It will be genuine, and it will indeed be felt and appreciated by others in your world and mine. Every thought and emotion is recorded in these realms. No love is lost.

* * *

An expanded consciousness is only a part of one's experience in the higher realms. We find it is impossible to describe in words the reality of these realms, but knowing of your interest, I will do my best to describe parts of this story. Realms Four and Five are really just a continuum of this expanding of consciousness. Personalities here interact on a regular basis with those who dwell in Realm Three as well as souls on Earth. Also they monitor the progress of those troubled ones in Realm Two.

Some of these "advanced" souls from Realms Four and Five decide to be reborn on the physical plane. This is usually done out of a desire to help others rather than to further one's own growth, although the latter naturally results from the former.

The nature of consciousness in these realms, Four and Five, is what I have attempted to describe in this chapter. There is an expansion of the mind, a uniting of personalities of like minds, to effect a greater whole and a larger mental existence. The opportunities for self-expression and self-fulfillment which arise from this larger-than-life self are arresting and delightful to those who dwell in these places. There is much interest in teaching others, and this is done in a direct way which you all understand intuitively but few understand consciously. This is a kind of shepherding of personalities. There has already been some writing on this subject, and several terms have been used for this phenomenon. Some of you on Earth understand that you have "spirit guides" on this side who watch over you and influence your thoughts. These spirit guides are also called "oversouls," a term which is somewhat more accurate. To my taste, "spirit guide" sounds like a creature emerging from the mists of a seance, ready to speak to you of ghosts and spooky happenings. An oversoul, on the other hand, implies a kind of exalted self, and a relationship of caretaking, which it is.

Be aware, these so-called spirits or oversouls are no more ghostly or less real than you are, sitting there in the flesh! In fact, if anything, they are more real. Their reality is more lively, more vital, more varied and full of emotion than you can even imagine. I do not mean that in a disparaging connotation toward you on Earth. I have a deep affection, admiration and the highest regard for your earthly reality. But by the same token, you should be open-minded about the reality of nonphysical beings. One does not require a body to truly exist. In many regards a body hampers one from existing to the fullest.

This relationship I am attempting to describe is at the foundation of your own earthly life. It is your own oversoul who urges you to be your best self. This oversoul is the author of your intuitions, your desires to do good and to be good. This oversoul is your own soul. Each man, woman and child of the Earth has a well-developed soul. Even though there are many confused conscious minds among people, there is a great wealth of intuitive wisdom available to all.

My secretary wonders why a wise oversoul would allow a personality to make such grave errors that he or she ends up in the darkness of Realm Two. The answer is simple. Individuals make their own decisions. They are free to do so. If they choose a path of selfishness, arrogance, hatred and meanness, then they cause their own suffering. Yet their own soul is good. Now this part is hard to explain, but each of you is a whole person, with your soul an integral part. Yet you are also separate, in that you can divorce yourself from your soul and move away from its wisdom. If you dwell in Realm Two, your good and wise soul continues to reside in the higher realms and attempts to bring you wisdom if you are receptive. Yet an individual in Realm Two can create his own small hell, all by himself, if he wants to. He will reside there until he feels truly that he has learned his lessons of humility, repentence and appreciation for others. So the soul is at once a part of you and separate from you.

To return to the main thread of this narrative: the oversoul, who resides in Realm Four or Five, then occupies much time and thought in watching over his or her earthly personalities, as well as helping friends in Realm Three. I mention earthly personalities in the plural, because usually an oversoul has four, five or six simultaneous Earth lives over which (s)he is guardian. This may seem shocking to some of you, yet it is supremely natural.

Remember that consciousness is larger in these stages and capable of handling more stimulus and information at once. You could compare it to a powerful computer, if you like, which can far outperform the simpler models. But this is no computer, for these oversouls, these large personalities, are filled with vitality and good heart.

The ramifications to you are these: as your soul or oversoul watches over you, (s)he simultaneously watches over several others on this Earth. This is most helpful to you as an individual. It means you are tied to other earthly experience at any given moment in time. You are not consciously aware of this influence, but you are aware of it subconsciously. This phenomenon has been called "counterpart personalities." Please understand this does not lessen the uniqueness or validity of you alone. It makes available to you on certain intuitive levels and in the sleep state a wealth of complementary Earth experience. Many of your dreams are a way of swapping information or exchanging anecdotes, so to speak, with your counterpart personalities. You may be actual friends with a counterpart or you may live at opposite ends of the Earth. Nevertheless, this is an example of the rich, varied creativity of consciousness and its desire to know itself to the fullest.

9 The Highest Realms

THIS is what our previous description has been heading toward: the farthest reaches of consciousness, the largest caches of wisdom. Where does one go when one's growth is the fullest possible?

And so I will describe, to the best of my abilities, the realities of Realms Six and Seven.

Since I myself reside in Realm Six, you would think I could

speak clearly about it. But as you might guess after reading the last chapter, this realm is most difficult to picture. It goes so far beyond your normal orientation, your highly focused consciousness identified with one physical body, as to be utterly incomprehensible to you. But I will do my best to give at least a glimpse of my world.

The vehicle of language in itself presents obstacles to the translation, because it is a linear progression, one word after the next. Therefore it can only present one idea at a time. My reality is a million ideas all at once. I am so vast that you can't even imagine me.

I have told Judy that my consciousness is approximately 100 times greater than hers, yet in actuality, my reality is much vaster than that. Too, she is not aware of her entire self, an enigma which is part of each of you.

In the previous chapter I told about the joining of consciousness. This linking up continues in my realm and the highest one, too. It is a part of our existence. But we are not just consciousnesses larger than those entities who reside in Realms Four and Five. There is a qualitative difference. This is reflected in our broader activities.

For example, at this moment as I dictate a book script to Judy Laddon on Earth, I also am monitoring activities on hundreds of other planets. I direct most of my efforts now to your galaxy, but I am also familiar with many others, and my influence is felt. Beyond that, there are activities which you could not relate to at all. Your physical world and your perception of it does not represent all there is to the universe. There are countless "alternate" physical universes which are simply on other vibrational codes than yours, and which you cannot perceive. What I am saying is this: I am a god in the universe. Yet I am not the highest.

The highest and largest consciousnesses are beyond my understanding by quite a bit, yet I interact with and am helped by them. They are actual entities, vast personalities, who reside in Realm Seven. Together, you could say they are God, or All-

That-Is. They understand and know this universe intimately, every tiny portion of it, and they can perceive all that happens in this universe.

I am referring to the inhabitants of Realm Seven in the plural, because I am aware of various distinct portions, but I know this may trouble some of you who are devotedly monotheistic. You can feel comfortable with your belief despite my words, because you can also refer to the residents of this highest realm as a single entity, God. Each part understands and knows all the other parts.

"We create worlds where you can find physical life...you yourselves create other consciousness."

Now, the activity which is shared in Realm Six and Realm Seven, but not in the other realms, is that of Creation. I mean this to have a capital C. We are talking big stuff here, not just the idea of creativity, painting or writing, or the larger creativity in Realm Three of creating thought-forms of flowers or buildings. I speak of creating worlds. Try to imagine this: with our desires and our understanding we create worlds where you can find physical life, sustenance and fulfillment. We give birth to galaxies, filled with stars, planets and vast reaches of new consciousness.

You are unaware of this, but you yourselves create other consciousness. In fact, most of the people on Earth were "created" by strong thoughts of human beings who existed eons before you. God creates the larger structure which sustains you all, and (S)He continues to create. There is no end to it.

I hate to burst the balloon of the Big Bang theorists—and Judy hates to hear me be so flippant—but there was no big bang, and there will be no contraction of matter as your scientists have postulated. The truth is, there is a continuation of evolution, with growth and change. The universe will continue to expand into eternity.

It is true that at one time—and there is a marked distortion in meaning by my attempt to formulate this huge idea into small words—there was no matter, there was no physical world. God existed, and there were vast realms of consciousness and personality. Because of God's desires to bring greater opportunities to His/Her offspring, physical worlds were created. This creation was simultaneous, all over the place, and did not occur from the explosion of one dense body.

Creation in your physical world—and we mustn't forget that yours isn't the only one—occurs in a different manner. Judy has asked me about the phenomenon of black holes, and I have told her that your astronomers are mistaken in their assumptions. These dense areas exist, but matter is not sucked into them. Matter emerges from them. These are growth points of your physical world. It is true that light does not penetrate their depth, for the density is immense. But matter emerges from them and fathers new worlds.

Now, then. It's pretty hard to describe God, but I think I've given you an inkling of the reality of Realm Seven. The interesting thing for you to note is actually twofold. From your point of view, as a physical being on Earth, you probably won't interact much with God on a direct basis. Don't misunderstand me, (S)He hears your prayers. But there are many fine souls who are guarding and guiding you, and God understands they can take care of you. There is no reason for God to interact directly. There are, however, many miracles which occur in your world, most of which you are completely unaware of. Usually you call these occasions coincidence or luck, but they are carefully orchestrated over here. The important thing is to know you are never alone. You are known intimately in these realms, and God knows of you. (S)He knows you have many guardians who are responsive to your needs and desires.

The other point of interest to you in this discussion of the highest realms is a reassurance to each individual that life and consciousness forever beckon one to further growth and understanding. In the eternity of spiritual existence, we have a wonderful and hearty enjoyment of ourselves and our fellow beings. We are not angels up here. In fact, we are not "up." We are just here, beside you, living in our different plane. And while you can't see us, we can see you. Your society's definition of Heaven is a gross misrepresentation. Heaven sounds like a deathly boring place to be, and I for one wouldn't be caught dead there. All the residents of these spirit realms have well-developed senses of humor, just like you do, perhaps more so. Our humor is never sarcastic, though, or at the expense of someone else. There are many ironies to laugh over and much spirited interchange among us all.

If you desire to slumber away eternity after you die, well, sorry, you're out of luck. You may sleep awhile, if you choose to, but then you'll wake up and have to get on with life! It is always fun, always a challenge to you, and filled with unutterable pleasures. You need not fear extinction of your ego or your personality. But you will change, even as you do now. This change is like a flower blooming; it is natural and beautiful.

My secretary has asked the ultimate question about growth in the spirit realms: does God continue to grow and change? Or is Realm Seven something like being forever in the 12th grade, or forever in graduate school? The answer, most assuredly, is no. There is always growth, even for God. Of course, God's growth is on an immense scale, impossible to think of. As I have mentioned, there continues to be joining of consciousnesses in Realm Seven. So a new sense of creativity, new identity, new understandings are continually entered into that realm as well as all others.

10	**The Role of Sex**

YOU were all wondering, I bet, if I would forget about this subject, which I so mischievously referred to awhile back. I know you all intimately, remember? I am aware of your acute interest in sexual relations between people and the role sexual identity plays for the individual. Without drafting a huge, psychological tome on the subject, I will make a few comments which I hope will be illuminating.

Basically, all souls are without sex. We haven't mentioned it yet because I wanted to put this in context, but in the many reincarnations you have all had in physical life, you have been born in both sexes. It is important to the development of individual character to experience physical life from various perspectives.

As you know, there are certain trademarks to the sexes that are thought to be distinguishing features. The male, by nature, is somewhat more physically aggressive, strong, outwardly oriented than the woman. The woman tends to be more gentle, intuitive, have greater ease in expressing and identifying her emotions. Both orientations, however, are shared by each personality, and the development of all these traits is essential to the well-rounded spiritual character.

Now, the physical interaction of the sexes is a special relationship created by God for your pleasure and growth. It is based upon the enduring longing that people have to be close to one another. Its purpose is the communion of souls on Earth. I naturally am referring here to sex in its ideal form, a physical, sensuous enjoyment of two people who are deeply in love.

I will also say, however, that we view sex very liberally in the spirit world. We are not ignorant of your natures, you know. The truth is, all sex is good. I am not speaking of sexual crimes or acts of meanness. I am speaking of the natural urgings that people have for one another, those earthly urges to be together physically. We know that these occasions are not always accompanied by an enduring love and are often quite transitory. But these couplings have greater purposes, beyond the physical gratification alone. They are always enriching to some extent. For one thing, they are a dependable source of fun, which is also important in your world.

If we spirits didn't approve of your sexual activity, then you wouldn't have so much of it, would you? Some of the urgings you feel so strongly come through your intuitions from this side. You are urged to enjoy life, enjoy your contemporaries and know them deeply. There is a special closeness which can only be achieved in your realm through this special act.

I have told Judy that all sex is good, in all circumstances. [With a few qualifications. —J.L.] Of course that includes in and out of marriage. In the case of "unwanted" babies, this is also true. You see, sexual expression is one of humankind's important freedoms and opportunities for learning. In this area as in all others, men and women are free to create their own experience; they are free to make mistakes and to learn from them. There are higher purposes to all human activity which you cannot perceive but which underly your world. Purposes of sexual intercourse fall into this category. You cannot perceive the full meaning of it, but it is full of importance, and you have full freedom to explore its meaning.

I would say to parents of adolescent children that the desire to love and be close to others is a wholesome urge. It should not be lumped into a broad category of Problems which parents must contend with. It is not comparable to crime, lethargy, drug usage and assorted other problem behavior in adolescents. It is an expression of wholeness and joy. You may not choose to encourage your youngster to sleep with others, but neither should you layer him or her with terrible guilt feelings about the impropriety of natural urges. You should remember, too, that your society artificially postpones conventionally accepted ages for marriage much beyond the biologically mature ages of 14 to 16 years.

From my point of view, I'd like to see more realistic attitudes in your society about the role of sex. The best thing a parent can do is to convey the great pleasure of sexual intercourse coupled with deep love and respect. This will help the young people be true to their intuitions to care about others and take care in their relationships. Concerns of emotional maturity, pregnancy and health should be shared by members of the family. If parents convey their loving interest and sympathy, then the adolescent will not leap into inappropriate relationships.

I'll answer another question which will naturally crop up in the reader's mind when pondering the life beyond. What about sex in the afterlife? Does that earthly pleasure fall by the wayside? Once again, is there no more fun to be had in a dull and stagnant heaven above? I am most pleased to make the following announcement: There is sexual pleasure over here, too! Of course! Anything of such great interest to you would not be abandoned in these realms. I will shock you once again, I'm sure, by saying that sexual interaction over here is much different, and much more fun, than anything you know on Earth. Your physical bodies are wonderful; I want to stress that. And your sexual organs are sensitive and capable of conveying great sensual pleasure. But the style of sexual interaction in Realms Three, Four and Five over here seems the highest possible sensual pleasure.

I'll give a brief description of how it works. The spirit body is composed of much finer stuff than the physical body. It carries the ability to sense pleasure only, not pain. The atoms which comprise the body are farther apart than your physical counterpart. When two entities desire to link up, to exchange sexual pleasure or energy, they merge, body to body. They become superimposed, one with the other, and exchange energy and emotion from one entire body to the other. Every cell interacts with a cell from the other. This creates an all-consuming perception of almost electrical or magnetic excitement and pleasure. It is far beyond the orgasm you know, and it brings souls together more intimately than is possible on your physical plane. So folks here have fun, too.

"The letters of my name I chose to symbolize the connection between your world and mine."

You have a lot to look forward to. But don't try to hurry over here. Life in the spirit realms cannot substitute for your earthly experiences. Earth living holds invaluable lessons for you and great joy in the process. Be heartened that man is immortal. You do not die when your physical body does. You are as enduring as the stars. Even more so.

A few last, provocative words about sexuality. Judy has asked me if I enjoy sex, and I answered yes. But I surprised her when I said it is not sexual interaction with other entities. It is interaction within myself, for I am a vast gestalt of personalities, and I create this exchange of energy within my own boundaries.

For the purposes of my own identity to you, I call myself "Af," and I refer to myself in the feminine gender. This I do for several reasons. I call myself Af not because that is my name; my identity is not associated with letters of the English alphabet. Those letters I chose to symbolize the connection between your world and mine. A, the first letter of your alphabet, corresponds to Realm One, physical life, and F, the sixth letter, corresponds to Realm Six, my reality.

Entities of my realm sometimes interact directly with personalities in Realms Three, Four and Five. On many occasions, it is helpful to my students or friends in those realms that I materialize into some kind of visible humanistic form. I often choose a feminine one in which I feel comfortable. But I am truly without sex, I am beyond sex, I am male as much as female. I am a vast consciousness beyond any definition you know.

There is another reason I refer to myself in the feminine, and that is to offset the terrible tradition in many of your societies of giving greater credence to the male identity. This is a sad state of affairs. Why must you set yourselves up, one against another? One sex better than another, one race superior, one nation better than all others? It is an absurdity which goes against the truths pervading all of the universe. Open your minds to the validity of all life around you. Open your minds to recognize goodness in its many forms, and do not force your stern judgments on everything which might deviate from your own narrow definitions of rightness. In the end, you merely create great difficulties for your own development, plus you make a misery of your life as you live it.

But if you can allow all other people to be themselves, and respect them for it, and share the good feelings which will pour forth from your own heart, then you create for yourself an accepting posture, an attitude that accepts others, that accepts life and that accepts the larger purposes which might be hidden from your understanding.

The universe is not chaotic. It is supremely ordered and tended. All is right in the world. You have only to be yourself to reap the greatest rewards of all.

11 Growth of the Spirit

MY SECRETARY wonders at the logic of this chapter heading, since our chapters to date have all been concerned with spiritual growth and spiritual orientation.

I make a separate chapter heading here to stress the key points we have covered, for we are drawing this narrative to a close.

Now, then. Your purpose in life is to grow in character. It is not to doggedly pursue that which your society says is your own self-interest, such as amassing wealth, building a "healthy" retirement, traveling at length or otherwise indulging in purely selfish pursuits. Your purpose, I say again, is to grow in character. This is done by focusing not on yourself but on those around you. It is ironic, but by attending to all those people of your acquaintance, by giving of yourself to these people and to your family, only then do you truly find yourself and establish your own firm identity.

The "identity crises" that young people have, for instance, occur because they only look within themselves as foundations of their actions. If they would stop focusing within and look with an open heart to those around them, then they would have no crises in deciding what to do with their lives. There would be open paths beckoning to them. They would see that they were needed by others for certain support.

There are apparent contradictions in this concept. People must look within themselves to discover, intuitively as well as intellectually, that course which they are meant to pursue. Some people, by looking outwardly, don't notice the needs of others around them, but instead see only their own desires for material gain. They desire more clothes, more jewelry, expensive cars, extravagant houses. Their "outward" looking brings them no closer to spiritual fulfillment than the adolescent who is completely wrapped up in an "inward" struggle with self-identity.

The purpose of every word of this entire narrative is to awaken in the reader an understanding and remembrance of his or her own purpose in this life. As an old ghost, a disembodied spirit with greater perspective, I implore each of you, for your own good and the good of your world, to listen to your own deeper instincts. Listen to your heart and be true to it. Question first impulses and selfish motives. Think them through, and only then take action. This will bring you greater joy and spiritual reward than any amount of self-indulgence. Give of yourself to others and you will know greater peace and joy than you ever thought possible.

Do not think I recommend an ascetic lifestyle. You have already learned that we up here wholly approve of your spirited sexual pleasure. Likewise, it pleases us to see you take pleasure in the beauties and enjoyment of your world, whether they are in tending a fine garden, eating well, dressing in nicely tailored clothing, enjoying the fruits of your society. But as many philosophers have urged in the past, these things should be taken in moderation. Moderate eating, drinking, playing; moderate in one's work and one's pleasure. The only thing you can be immoderate in, with complete impunity, is your devotion to your own higher goals. Dictated by an inner impetus, these goals are familiar to each of you and should not be confusing. People know right from wrong when they truly seek understanding.

You may wonder about the crackpot who insists, "God told me to kill." This person heard a different voice and followed the evil urging only by ignoring the deeper instincts to be generous, kind and loving to others.

The distorted values in your society cause much moral confusion which we are saddened to witness. But remember this, it is not true that you go around only once in this life. So your purpose is not to grab all the gusto you can. You go around scores of times, and you are meant to become radiant spiritual beings by the end of your Earth incarnations. Don't despair that you may have far to go.

You don't need to receive credit on Earth for your good deeds and good thoughts. All action and all motivation are recorded in the vast realms of the universe, and you are known for what you truly are. Go about your life quietly, not seeking attention and admiration from others, but seeking to enrich others by your sincere interest and help. You will be amply rewarded by the satisfactions to your soul while in this life and when you reach the next.

For now, I bid you each a fond and hearty good day, full of the gusto of life and eternity.

Your interested friend,

—Af

BEDOUIN STORIES

Part Two

Twenty individual life stories, told by a "nonphysical" personality called Bedouin, are examined from a spiritual viewpoint with lessons for our times.

Preface to Bedouin Stories

IT SEEMS apt to mention that before Af got going with book dictation, when I was still occupied with personal sessions and answers to myriad questions, I was introduced to another personality who calls himself Bed, short for Bedouin. He reported that he had last lived in the 3rd century A.D. and that we were going to be writing books together.

Sure enough, when Af and I were finished with her portion of *Beyond the Veil*, Bed stepped forward and began dictation of the following section. I was disappointed at the start for several reasons. Bed seemed to be a nice enough fellow, but I didn't sense either the strength or the affection that I felt when talking to Af. Even so, Af acted as a mistress of ceremonies; she always spoke to me first when I began to take dictation. For example, after I sat down to receive a session, relax and open my mind, normally Af said hello to me, commented on any questions or problems I have had, then introduced Bed. Bed in turn made a few personal remarks and then said we were to begin book dictation. The pace I found to be more halting than with Af.

At first I didn't appreciate the following stories, which were written in 1982, but in time I was pleased with their many insights for modern life.

—J.L.

Introduction

I AM an "entity" residing in Realm Four who wishes to speak to your world. I have watched your Earth for centuries from my spiritual world. I clearly remember experiencing human lives, and I am deeply empathic with you now living. The stories I wish to tell may prove helpful to each of you in your own orientation to life.

My messages differ from Af's in several important regards. Af's book has been concerned with portraying the largest and furthest reaches of consciousness. She has attempted to prepare the reader for what can be expected after death when one enters these realms of spirit. Naturally, this information makes you sensitive to the type of life you are living now. But the main thrust of her work is to convey the greater realities which go far beyond your very finite and limited physical plane.

The stories which I wish to tell, and there are 20 of them, are short (sometimes very short) synopses of individual and actual lives which have been lived on Earth. (Names have been changed to protect the dead and living of these stories.) These accounts should help the reader gain perspective in evaluating his or her own life. In some cases, these prototypal cases may sound almost uncannily precise in their likeness to yourself or someone you know. This is, of course, an intentional effect of the material. You are meant to identify with these classic examples of living styles, thought habits, and motivations. This recognition ought to help you prepare to turn over a new leaf in your thoughts about your life and your environment.

A re-orientation of many in your society will be necessary in order to avoid the problems you now face. And for those who wish to preserve the status quo, I would like to point out the obvious: your society is deeply troubled, and these troubles spring from the spiritual illness which runs rampant over your Earth. You must all be aware you perch on the brink of a nuclear holocaust which would destroy the entire planet. We on

72

this side wonder when the killing will stop. The most conventional thinking of nations is to turn to warfare at the first threat from another nation. Warfare shows the greatest weakness, not strength, of a nation, for it shows a people without recourse, without spiritual strength or wisdom, without respect or regard for all human life, with only the most narrow definition of human value and achievement.

We are the ones praying for your enlightenment. We are the ones asking the gods what to do to help your world. It is our misery in watching your folly that helps to bring such a lofty entity as Af to your aid. To us, Af is like a great leader, a spiritual presence so vast and good that her reassuring and beautiful aura can encompass our entire world. We go to Af as you go to a president or chief of a great nation, with awe and respect and, unlike what you may feel for earthly authority, a complete trust.

It was Af—Judy didn't know this—who urged me to prepare these stories to dictate to Judy. And Af helped to train me in making this transmission possible. I am a novice in bridging this gap, in spanning planes. I have never before transmitted my own messages in such an orderly, consistent manner as that required for a book manuscript. But Judy has a great and abiding interest in receiving this material. Plus, she has a faith in the existence of us spirits who are good and wise in our realm, a faith that heartens us and gives us hope for your world. You can help to change the course of events which could destroy your world. It is attitudes, not bombs, which threaten your world with nuclear weaponry, and it is attitudes, not unrelated economics, which threaten to dehumanize you in your lifestyles.

Attitudes are just your own thoughts. You have control over these thoughts. You should evaluate what you have always assumed was the truth about life, and make sure you are not blindly accepting fallacies. The stories I am about to relate will reveal many of the accepted fallacies of your time.

DESERT VILLAGER
1 | From Student to Teacher

IT BEGAN over a thousand years ago, in a village in Turkey. This is the story of my last life on Earth and what has happened to me since that time. To Judy, the Earth medium who translates my story into a physical book for you to read, I call myself Bed, actually short for Bedouin. She doesn't think much of the name, inappropriate as it is by the standards of English names. But I believe it will suffice for our purposes here.

Judy doesn't go into a trance to receive these dictations from me, and as I myself am a little rusty in such procedures, we are groping our way along, trying to get comfortable. To you I'm just a long-forgotten nobody of a man who lived too long ago to worry over. The purpose of telling my story is to shed some light on the idea of survival of the spirit.

Naturally, if I am writing this book, and I do not exist physically on Earth, and I am not Judy's subconscious mind chattering away, then it must be true that the spirit can exist without the body. I know there are many who would not discount the possibility that Judy, through some kind of tricky ESP, receives these words without an actual personality dictating them to her as I do now. She herself continues to doubt the validity of this actual occurrence. But she also has faith that there is reason and justice to the world, that bodies do not create spirits, and that the soul is eternal. So if we can all refrain from pronouncements or judgments as to what is real at this time, then I'll get on with my story.

We are having some trouble deciding where "Bedouin" refers, but I think we are safe to say it is what you now call the Middle East, or Turkey specifically. I lived in this region in the 3rd century after Jesus Christ. I was aware of his teachings, by the way, but that is another story which we won't delve into right now. I was not too religiously inclined, nor were most of my

75

contemporaries.

I was born male in that life, to simple peasant parents, and we lived in a small village near a vast desert. While the terrain may have seemed, on the surface, to have been bleak, we actually had an abundance of food. There was a river near the village; we ate dates, grape leaves and fruit, raised sheep and had an abundant, simple life. The contrasts to your lifestyle in modern-day America are very marked, and I will explain what I mean by saying that yours is not necessarily the superior lifestyle. By giving up the simplicity of the farmer, the shepherd and the close ties of village life, modern humans have set before themselves certain obstacles to their own understanding. It is true you have much greater material wealth, but this has also been accompanied in many cases by a spiritual confusion.

Ah, but I am not a spiritual preacher coming to sermonize and put you all to sleep. I only wish to tell a little story about a simple man who lived long ago. This section is an autobiography, although it has little to do with the earthly writer, Judy Laddon. Her only relationship to me is this: we have been colleagues in these spirit realms and friends in lives past. We are not tied now psychologically, except that I have chosen her as a receptive vehicle to convey my little stories to your world. My fondness for the Earth and you who dwell there is very great. I feel your culture can benefit by greater contact with and belief in my realm. So, on with the tale.

While our lives were basically simple, they were full of pleasures and of love. Our family and our village were close-knit and happy. Although I married at an early age, set up housekeeping in a clean little hut and enjoyed the boisterous company of my three children, yet I felt great urgings to understand more about life. Our village had a tradition of folklore and accepted wisdoms, and neighboring villages, too, had similar histories to draw from. Also, we had heard about the teachings of Christ, yet in our culture the idea of one God was not accepted. Nevertheless I yearned to learn more and, in still young manhood, set out for a distant monastery for a period of study and reflection. Monasteries were repositories of written traditions and the closest thing we had to schools. I was determined to be gone just a short time, and bade my wife and children a fond farewell.

It was required that I travel across a portion of the desert, which I did with some trepidation. There were always dangers in such travel, and I was alone, without an accompanying caravan, since it was not a regular trade route. Nevertheless, I arrived at the monastery safely and was accepted by the monks most graciously to learn their way of life and thought.

At first there was some difficulty, since I did not know how to read, but this was accomplished with some speed, as I was much devoted to learning my lessons. In payment for my studies, I helped the monks in their labors of the field and in tidying quarters and preparing food. I sorely missed my family at first, but the excitement of the new lessons was so great that this was overcome. Too, I was aware my family was well provided for in their small but self-sufficient community.

The monastery housed collections of esoteric teachings and wisdom that dated back many centuries. Some of the origins of these teachings were unknown, yet their truth was apparent to the monks who acted as caretakers of the old manuscripts and tablets.

My studies first covered subjects which related to our current lives: the seasons, astronomy, planting and harvesting, mathematics and other practical lessons. Then, as the months passed, I was instructed in the more secret of the teachings: philosophy, telepathy, healing and religion. I was utterly captivated and planned to stay at the monastery until I had absorbed all the monks could teach me. On their part, these gentle teachers responded to my yearnings and took me in as one of them. I felt some remorse at the thought of not returning soon to my young family, but I could not quiet the passion I felt for this new knowledge.

Much of what I learned in those ancient days is gone. The

teachings are lost to modern times, and it is a sad loss, for your world could much benefit by them. At any rate, I will attempt here to cover some of the basic lessons I learned from that old school, lessons which can help you today as they helped me back then.

First of all, to love one another, that is the most basic of all of life's lessons. It is a truth which underlies your world on Earth and our world of spirit. It is easier said than done, of that we are all aware. Many people walk the face of the Earth thinking of no one but themselves, and they are hard to love, for they do not give out love in return. But they, more than kinder souls even, need love shown them as an example. They will respond to love, like a plant responds to light, and they can learn from it. This was a first lesson the monks taught me, and I knew it was true. The truth of it made me regret some of my past actions, but I felt a new hope in finally understanding clearly this universal message.

The monks described how this truth was ever apparent in the spirit world and how the sense of love from above could be felt by all. As you might guess, several of the monks were clairvoyant and clairaudient and directly perceived the realm of spirit, even while they wore their physical bodies. They were also adept at out-of-body projections and ventured into other realms quite easily. When they would return, they shared with others what they had learned in their astral travels.

While all this may sound farfetched, it really is quite ordinary. People are equipped to have this kind of perception. They just at present have mostly forgotten about it, and the many misconceptions of your society have not helped you to remember. We are amazed, for instance, that so many of your world do not believe, even, that the spirit survives physical death. Yet this is a basic truth. It is the basis of all the world's great religions. Can one study scripture and not get a sense of the eternal nature of spirit? I do not mean to praise your religions too much here, because they all have gross fallacies intertwined with their wisdom, and these have caused great suffering.

The monks taught a way of breathing which facilitates meditative alterations of consciousness, a shallow yet broad breath which aids in relaxation and aids in opening the chakras of the body. Your modern study of yoga retains some of these teachings, although others are lost.

During one of my out-of-body experiences I visited my wife and children and found that the youngest, a girl, was quite sick with fever. I tried to use my newly discovered healing powers from a distance on her but was not having any luck. So I set out for home in order to help this child, who by then was about eight years old. At that time I had been absent from home about five years, and I felt ready to return even though sad to leave the good monks. They had become like brothers to me, and we all felt a special bond of closeness.

Upon returning home, I found my young daughter had died, and I was stricken with remorse. I could not forgive myself for being absent for such a long period and somehow felt I could have helped the child to live. My wife, however, was very pleased to see me and glad for our family to be as one again. We mourned but a short time for the dead child. Then I began to introduce my wife and other children to the mysteries I had learned during my studies. They were very willing pupils and eager to know all.

There was naturally some resistance to new ideas which contrasted greatly with old ones. For instance, the idea of equality for all people, including women, was new. But it made sense and was met with much open-mindedness. The teachings I recounted regarding certain other lessons, such as healing and tales of the afterlife, were more readily accepted since they complemented the people's historical philosophy.

I refer to myself as a Bedouin, but we were not a wandering tribe in those days. We had a sense of security and a fondness for the countryside where our villages were built. We did not come under Roman rule; we were small enough that Rome was not even aware of our existence.

I continued to experiment on my own with altered states of perception, and I became adept at out-of-body journeys. During these trips, I naturally sought my daughter in the spirit realms to see how she was faring. I found her safe and sound and growing up rapidly. [It is said that children who die remain as children on the other side but that they grow up quickly. They are nurtured and taught by loving souls who have chosen to help them.]

Before long, I could see she was fully grown, and she communicated to me an understanding of her own early death. She died, she told me, to draw me into a greater understanding of the spirit realms, which could then be incorporated into my teachings. She herself was an advanced soul and needed no further Earth lessons. Her early death caused such acute and passionate emotions for me that it was helpful in spurring me on to greater understanding.

My people believed in many gods, many spirits all around us governing the forces of the Earth. They did not have a clear picture of a single, great God underlying all the universe, nor did they necessarily embrace the notion of survival of the human personality as it exists on Earth. The monks had access to great wisdoms from ages past which taught the truth about these matters.

Our own people, the Bedouins of that era, were without such a cultural history and had a more primitive understanding of the spiritual forces around us. So my teachings, which correlated with lessons reintroduced by Christ just three centuries before, were much respected. In my simple way I was able to improve the understandings among people in our village, as well as improve relationships with neighboring villages. Wives and husbands viewed each other with greater regard and love. Neighbors felt a little more generous and kindly toward one another. There grew a greater sense among all people that their lives had purpose, that their thoughts and actions would be reflected in the afterlife, and that what is sown on Earth is reaped after physical death.

I was content for the rest of my days in the satisfactions of our small community. And after my own death, it became clear to me that I had greatly fulfilled my own purpose in life. I had embraced universal truths and had lovingly communicated them to others. I adjusted easily to the next realm of spirit. It was shown me that I had learned enough lessons in that life, plus the many previous incarnations I had lived through, to be able to pass beyond the stages where it was necessary to continue with further Earth incarnations.

* * *

In Judy's previous work with Af, we have heard of the various realms of spirit. To refresh the memory, I will recount here what one can expect upon passing across the threshold called death.

You are spiritual beings, whether you think of yourselves like that or not, who are in the most restrictive realm, the physical world. We can call this Realm One. Realm Two is the first of the nonphysical realms, and it is the one where confused, disturbed and troubled souls find themselves after their unfulfilled physical lives have ended. Usually in these regions reside those who have been overly selfish and mean-spirited. This realm would correspond with your ideas of Hell. But is should be stressed that there is no such thing as eternal damnation, and that all souls are basically good. Growth is inevitable, even if it takes ages, literally. Realm Three is the first of the so-called realms of light. This is where I found myself after death following my last physical incarnation. Beyond this, there are Realms Four, Five, Six and Seven. I will not cover them at length now; I will just say that the highest, Realm Seven, is God or All-That-Is. Between here and there is an unbelievable wealth of growth, wisdom, spirited activity, creative consciousness and love. In Realm Four, where I now reside, personalities can confront their previous incarnations on Earth and evaluate their overall spiritual progress. Too, they connect up, in an inexplicable way, with others of like minds, and therefore have greater capacity for understanding and perception.

Our definition of these realms of spirit should help give you an idea of what happens to personalities between their Earth lives, and even after they have ended physical reincarnation altogether.

The aim of this volume of stories is to give actual examples of Earth lives and the purposes served for those personalities who experienced them.

I lived, all in all, over 500 lives, and from each one I learned something important.

A first observation, you might notice, is the paltry few years, the small sum of time, which a soul spends in any one life. That is why so many lives are undertaken, one after another. Do not feel your existence must be justified by the actions of your single life. The greatest lesson is simply to do your best, and be your best toward others, as is humanly possible.

Your actions and thoughts toward others are of the greatest importance. For they indicate and determine your own spiritual growth, as well as give you the opportunity to be of assistance to others in your realm.

In Realm Four I am linked with many other entities or personalities with whom I share my own consciousness. This makes me bigger, not less, for I too share their thoughts and impulses, and our lives are very full and vital. You would be surprised to know of us, and you would find our reality fascinating.

Judy worries we may make a terrible goof in our reports and cause this work to be discredited as utterly false and impossible. [In a personal Af session, I was told, "You wonder if you are getting this new material right, and you hope your account won't clash with historical Earth records. We laugh with you at the irony of this worry. We have just finished an entire book section on the spirit realm, and you had no such worry. As soon as we enter your terrain, so to speak, you are concerned you may have your facts crossed." —J.L.]

But I am not worried about scholars. They should drop their scholarly robes and pretenses in order to listen to the truths within their own hearts. My little stories could help them learn lessons of their own.

My last few lives were really pinnacles of my own development, but that is not always the case with Earth lives. It happens sometimes that souls choose a last life that is merely a rest from the drama and passions of previous lives—perhaps not even particularly fulfilling—but nonetheless the last life chosen. This is perfectly normal. Unlike the reincarnational misconceptions of some of your religious thinkers, the last Earth life lived is not necessarily saintly. It may be very ordinary indeed. And the end of Earth incarnations does not bring a soul into oneness with God but merely into a richer learning environment with new opportunities for growth.

From this point in our script I would like to recount specific lives which have been lived on Earth and look at what those souls thought about their lives after they reached spirit. These examples are acquaintances of mine, or personalities I have known directly. They are not fictitious—just the names are—and they are meant to illustrate common experiences among humans.

2 | CIVIL WAR SOLDIER
Learning Love from Battle

HENRY was a woodworker at the time of the Civil War. From his shop in Virginia, he made cabinetry and furniture, and did finish work in fine houses. Because of his careful craftsmanship, he was a prosperous man before the war started. During the war, he took up arms and suffered great emotional stress in witnessing the bloody, crazy conflict which divided households against one another. This war experience was jarring to his nature and caused certain changes to his personality.

When Henry saw the division caused by contrasting attitudes in otherwise close and loving families, and there were many in that category, he had a sudden rush of insight. He saw his own life to date as being emotionally pale, not vital at all. His interest had been aimed at material acquisition and not on building loving relationships. An unmarried man without close loved ones, he experienced a change of heart by witnessing the cold horrors of war. They symbolized for him the coldness of his own life and the way he had hidden himself from others.

Although he fought on the winning side, he felt little pleasure in the victory. In fact, Henry thought the war itself was an awful mistake, that there should have been a civilized resolution to the philosophical disparities of his time.

But he was grateful his own life was spared, and he returned to civilian life with new gusto and new purpose. He determined to be more generous with his craft and to be more friendly with others. As a result, he became a popular and much-loved man in his community. He married rather late in life but with much mutual affection, and he and his wife had several children. With his actions and his words toward others he conveyed charity, humility, generosity and warmth. His life ended leaving him much fulfilled and at peace with himself.

* * *

This little vignette is a revealing one for a couple of reasons. Many of your society focus too much on material acquisition and personal gain. This is a grave error from a spiritual viewpoint, for it is grounded in selfishness and egotism, not a spirit of giving to others. The drive behind this acquisitiveness comes from the base desire to set oneself above others, to capture some measure of superiority. This goes against the urgings of the heart, which are to share one's plenty and give generously to all around you.

Another lesson from this story of an actual man is the power of contrasts in teaching lessons. Quite often a shocking or disturbing experience is chosen by a soul to emphasize an important lesson. Therefore many good lessons are learned in wars, or in crippling illnesses, or accidents, or many other types of events. This reasoning does not justify wars—we on this side are always saddened by such inhuman behavior, such an immoral reaction to problems. But the lessons of war are dramatic nonetheless, and combat often awakens in men's breasts their own deepest longings for love of their brothers, the need for kindness among men, the true purposes of physical life.

So, you might say, this soul was "saved" by his war experience, for his prior life had been shallow and selfish. Had he not "seen the light," his departure from the physical would have found him in an impoverished state in the spiritual realm, and his make-up lessons would have been difficult and long. To change his ways and his spiritual orientation while still living was a blessing to his soul, and created for him many joys, both in his earthly life and in the hereafter.

3 | POOR SEAMSTRESS Generosity

LINDA was a seamstress in the 1920s in America. Her life was one of apparent deprivation and poverty, but in actuality it was rich and rewarding. She was kindhearted, humble and generous to all around her. She had many children, yet managed to give an abundance of love and concern to each of them. Though she worried often about earning enough money to feed her family, she yet remained cheerful in her heart and empathic to her family and friends. She did not begrudge her circumstances but accepted them as her lot in life and gave thanks to God for her many blessings. Upon death, she reaped the many rewards in the spirit realm that were her due after such an exemplary life.

This short life synopsis holds many valuable lessons for your time. With your labor unions and focus on the business world, your society has encouraged egotistical thinking. It is true the original impetus behind labor unions was to block the exploitation of workers by ruthless employers, yet the main orientation today is one of workers always striving to get more for themselves. As you can see, the idea aims at getting, not giving. This is a crucial philosophical and emotional fulcrum. Individuals compare their own material circumstances to those of other people and are driven to acquire always more. They view employers as fountains of perceived benefits to themselves, rather than as partners in social transactions, the production of whatever goods or services they are involved in. This orientation is destructive and is now causing some of the economic and social dislocation that you all are perceiving.

People in Western society could learn much from the poor seamstress we just described. Poverty and economic struggle are not to be disdained. They can aid in learning spiritual lessons. Poverty is a powerful tool in encouraging humility in some cases. On the other hand, we are dismayed at your society's penchant

86

for equating material wealth with personal distinction.

You should recognize that your definition of poverty, and the context in which I now use the term, is not a universal one. The poor of your society would be thought materially well-off in a more primitive society. What we think of as true poverty is a matter of the soul. There is much true poverty in the United States, many impoverished souls, even amid unprecedented material wealth.

The simple and gracious life of Linda the seamstress should be an example to all of the wealth of the spirit. Her soul sought the lessons of that life, and she learned them beautifully. She gave abundantly, though she had little materially to offer, to all around her—family, friends and clients. She was always cheerful, gracious and concerned about others. She did not begrudge her circumstances, though her work was long and hard; she never took a vacation, and she was often uncertain about her next meal. Yet she accepted that her life had a greater meaning, she had faith that she would be provided for in a large sense and she relished the fond relationships which encompassed her life.

* * *

You should not focus on the injustices you might believe surround you but instead on your gifts and the miracle of life. See the many people around you as living opportunities for your kindness, and give of yourself generously. If you encounter hardships or obstacles in your life, recognize that these carry deeper meanings; they are intended to challenge you and to test your spiritual strength. Rise up to meet them. Do not become mired by them and despondent over your perceived shortcomings.

Each life has a divine purpose, you might say, and each person is given a spiritual challenge to meet in life. We do not exhort you to be martyrs or to eschew the material comforts which are available to you. We simply point out that they are not ends in themselves. If an individual spends a lifetime feathering his or her own nest and largely ignoring others, then that person has missed the point of life. The soul is endlessly encouraged to become greater, to open itself up, to put selfish concerns aside and give one's energies and affections to others. This is the great spiritual challenge of all physical life, and each person is encouraged to meet this challenge in his or her own individual manner.

4	**BOOKKEEPER** **Money First**

CHARLES was a bookkeeper in the U.S. in the early 1800s. He worked in a bank office performing rote clerical and accounting tasks. His goal in life was to set aside enough money to retire easily in old age without fears. His dreams came true, as far as they went, but it was a pitiful life in retrospect. His whole world revolved around a great regard for money. He was married, with two children, but his affections did not run deeply for any of his family. He was fascinated by his job and grew to place tremendous weight upon the power of money. He was totally ignorant of the true purposes of life and completely misguided in his personal aims.

This does not mean that this man was abandoned by his own soul, or was not urged by his intuitions to participate in life more fully. He simply was restricted by his own small thinking. His heart would urge him to show greater love to his wife and children, and Charles would push aside such thoughts as weak, unmanly, sentimental. He was coldhearted. Although not outwardly cruel or mean to others, for the most part he was indifferent to those around him.

At various times in his life, Charles was intuitively urged to develop his talents in new directions. At each urging, he suppressed his true desires and became more intensely determined about what he perceived was his best course: to accomplish the clerical tasks at his job expertly—and honestly, I might add—and to fuss over his own personal financial status. His eventual retirement and old age were materially comfortable, as he had hoped. But he was joyless, like he had been throughout his earlier years. Charles had developed no abiding human ties. His family found it difficult to be loving to such an old codger, and he had no caring friends to speak of. His former colleagues at the bank felt no bond with him. His final years were lonely and frustrating because he couldn't understand what was missing in the life he had so carefully planned and executed.

When Charles died and surprised himself by surviving in the spirit world, he was quite amazed to review his life with new eyes. He was shocked to see he had missed literally all his opportunities for spiritual growth. His life had been a setback; instead of advancing, his soul had been thwarted and diminished at every turn.

He could not blame society for his failures since he fully accepted and even exaggerated certain values commonly held in his culture. Charles was confused by the rush of insight he encountered. He understood the rudiments of his problem but not the entire picture. He was aware that he had died and that he was wrongly focused in his life. The very existence of his continued consciousness in the spiritual realm contradicted firmly held beliefs, mainly that physical life was all there is and that material gain was the pinnacle of achievement. So he was grappling from the start of his rebirth on this side with philosophical dilemmas. Too, he had been shown a tantalizing glimpse of unutterable worlds of beauty over here and allowed to realize that these worlds beckoned him to enter when he was ready.

But then he found himself inside a filthy, unattractive hovel of a dwelling. Although his spirit body could not register pain or hunger, still he felt chilled to the bone, figuratively, by his impoverished environment. He found he was unable to leave this house and also unable to tidy it up. Charles was trapped, and he didn't at first understand that his own small-mindedness had created his surroundings. Nor did he know that his own thoughts and desires held the key to his release from this lonely ugliness. Periodically, visitors would stop to offer their assistance and sympathy. But Charles received them coldly, envying them their freedom and conveying bitterness about his own circumstances.

He tortured himself in this manner for a long time. This was for Charles a period of atonement. He was suffering, by a kind of unconscious choice, in order to do penance for his poorly lived physical life. Deep in his heart he understood that each physical life is a blessing and a gift. A wasted life is a shame indeed. Too, a wasted life has created a void, for it has robbed another soul, who might have entered that life more fruitfully, of the cherished Earth experience. There are many other entities waiting to enter Earth at the earliest opportunity, and a failed life is a sorry waste which translates as lost opportunity to others.

So his deepest, though hidden, understanding led Charles to a long and difficult experience, penance for his wrong orientation and poor thinking during physical life. Charles' mind remained closed until his lessons had truly sunk in, until he was thoroughly convinced of his own poor circumstances and poor actions in life and was ready to learn anew the great truths of the universe.

Then, and only then, did he begin to see the light. It dawned on him that he had been a wretched person by ignoring those around him; that in life he had, time and again, pushed aside his own best impulses in favor of mean ones; that his obsession with money and material wealth had blinded him to the glories all around which spring from the beauty and abundance of the Earth and her creatures, and which pour forth from the human heart.

As he began to understand such matters, little by little his small world changed. At first it appeared that his dwelling was less filthy and impoverished, and his occasional visitors lingered a bit to say a few words. Then as he began to seek advice and even help, with a more open mind and open heart to those who made themselves available to him, he began to perceive actual comfort and solace in his dwelling. It appeared cleaner, the furnishings more comfortable, and the atmosphere decidedly warmer.

His progress from that point was steady and rewarding. It had only required an open mind on his part and an eagerness for interaction with others. Too, his progress required a certain new humility for Charles, for his adherence to false ideals on Earth had created a proud rigidity. This had to be laboriously chipped away before he could make any progress on this side. Pride and arrogance are anathema to growth of the spirit.

To summarize, Charles' Earth life earned him his just reward in spirit: he found himself in impoverished circumstances in Realm Two. Not the worst of circumstances by a long shot, but clearly impoverished nonetheless. Yet with effort and after quite a bit of mental suffering he rose out of his situation to learn again what his soul had known always. After much inner searching and a difficult path, Charles eventually emerged into the beautiful world of Realm Three, where with joy he has undertaken work which furthers his own growth and contributes to others. He yet has many debts to pay from his last life, and he is eager to repay them on Earth, that great testing ground.

But he must wait his turn to be reborn, and that waiting in itself is a further burden he carries as graciously as he can. The decades pass, and still he must wait. He understands that no matter how pleasant and fulfilling his "spirit" life may be, still he has an appointment with fate which cannot be ignored. He must return to physical life if he is to fully surpass his grave errors of the life now past. This is part of the pervasive justice of the universe. It is not a cruel justice, but full of love, mercy and joy. The universe records every thought and impulse of every human life, and these either will work to forward the spiritual growth of an entity, or they work against such growth. To atone for one's mistakes, the soul does not skip any steps. This atonement is chosen by the individual, not thrust upon him by an outside force.

5 | THE MAID AND HER JESTER
Contagious Love

MARY was a maid in a medieval court. She was married to the court jester, and between them they provided an abundant livelihood and much appreciated services in the royal court. They felt all their dreams had come true, except one. They were childless and were saddened by this void. Yet they continued with their work and their own loving relationship.

The love they had for each other was passionate and deep. It broadened their hearts, colored their lives and influenced their attitudes toward other people. While their own material needs were adequately met, still they felt humble about themselves and generous with their friends and acquaintances. Where they perceived injustice or real want in their community, they attempted to correct it.

When these good souls died, they found themselves in the joyous realms of light, in Realm Three. They had learned well their lessons in life and had opened their hearts to others, so their transition to spirit was easy and full of glad surprises.

I am telling this particular little story to illustrate several points. First of all, the love between men and women is natural and good. Even though there are many misunderstandings about these relationships, we on this side view them with wholehearted approval. Between lovers, for instance, sex is always good. Always. (I speak here of those who love each other, not necessarily those involved in casual sex.) Beware of judging others, of pronouncing judgments on another's morals because he or she has loved another out of wedlock or one too young or too old. Love is expansive. Sexually expressed love helps the soul to know itself and to have the deepest kind of communion with another. To link spirits and bodies together, this act and this relationship are beautiful to behold.

There is another lesson to this little story. I have purposely set

92

it in a time period, the Middle Ages, which is foreign to you. You of the 20th century do not feel connected to centuries past, but you are. Nearly all of you now living also lived in these former times. You have known scores of other lives in dozens of historical periods. My example here is to show the universal concerns of physical incarnation. Whatever the historical period, the basic lessons the soul seeks to understand are the same. Regardless of historical time frame. Regardless of nationality, sex, race. The human experience is a common one.

Too, we on this side view your modern world with eyes very different than those of your own experts and analysts. The modern 20th century citizen of "developed" nations does not represent a pinnacle of development, certainly not of spiritual enlightenment. As most of you are so painfully aware, the rapid technological growth has not made great contribution to either human happiness or international peace. On the contrary, in many instances your technology has thwarted that which it was created to resolve.

Another lesson to be learned by this story of Mary the maid and her husband relates to their childless state. They were good-hearted and fulfilled people. Why did they have no children, which they so ardently desired? When they reached this side, all was made clear; there are great purposes to life, and all life situations have deeper meanings. They were repaying karmic debts by their denied desire for children. In a previous incarnation together, they had a very large family and had not devoted the love and attention that each child deserved and yearned for. As parents, they had taken for granted their many blessings, their many fine children, and so they were denied these blessings in their next incarnation.

As they reviewed their progress and their lives from the larger perspective gained on this side, they were pleased at their childlessness, for through that suffering they had fully repaid the debt owed due to a poor orientation in a previous life.

None of my readers should conclude that all current hardships or deprivations are karmic in nature or necessary to the development of the spirit. It is true there are psychic constructs underlying all physical events and that karmic history directly affects your world. But you are not meant to witness the sufferings of others complacently, saying, "Well, they must have been naughty in a past life, so their suffering is justified." You are meant to offer help to one another. To feed one another, offer shelter, clothing, companionship and affection. Modern medicine is also good in many of its aspects; so we from this side are pleased to see childless couples receive medical help to correct their problems.

<table>
<tr><td>6</td></tr>
</table>

ENGLISH SAILOR
6 Becalmed

JAMES was an English sailor in the 1700s. He worked on board merchant ships traveling from Britain to America and other ports. This was a difficult but interesting life to James and others in that line of work. Being divorced from the land for long periods was disorienting, but many came to feel more at home on rocking decks than on dry land. Too, sailors were apart from their women folk and had to constantly thwart their special longings for family life and womanly love. Emotionally, these men's lives left much to be desired. Their circumstances forced them into long periods of celibacy, little tender or warm contact with others, and a kind of constant male bravado that was grinding to their morale.

James had a wife and a new baby in London when his ship sank in a storm and he perished. He was a young man who had lived a short, apparently awkward life. Why did his larger soul choose for him to die?

When he reached this side, James fully realized the appropriateness of his death. His continued life would have held little opportunity for his own further spiritual growth. His economic circumstances favored his continuation as a sailor, and he had learned sufficiently from that lifestyle in his years on the oceans. His wife was apart from him for such extended periods that she hardly knew him, and his death therefore was not a hardship to her and the baby. It was not a traumatic journey for James to come over the threshold of death. He soon found contentment, peace and new challenges over here.

The purpose of this short recounting is a simple one: an individual life does not have to be greatly rewarding from an emotional standpoint to have well served its purposes nonetheless. James was true to himself during his life. He was kind, courteous and respectful of other people, yet his heart did not overflow with love. In fact, his heart was often rather closed to his surroundings, and his existence was often a shallow and rote performing of required duties.

In a long line of physical reincarnations, James' life as a sailor had been a short but poignant one. It emphasized the value of human communication, human love at the most intimate levels and the grounding effect of the physical earth. To spend one's life floating over the seas, adrift emotionally and physically as well, is a poor excuse of a life. I do not mean to indict sailors here at all. As the reader can see, James' life was indeed a good one for him. But its primary benefit was one of contrast, for it created a dramatic departure from previous, richer lives by accentuating the undesirability of emotional isolation. Many souls choose such a life occasionally. Some become priests or nuns and live within a confined area, interacting only impersonally and formally with those around them. Others become hermits or recluses and remove themselves even further from human intercourse. James chose the accepted variation on this theme in the 1700s of being a merchant seaman, caught up in the rigorous chores of the sailing vessel, achieving only a guarded camaraderie with the other sailors he journeyed with, drifting from port to port until his own life support, the vessel which physically transported him over the waters, collapsed on the shifting oceans of the planet.

It was appropriate he should die on the sea, and such was the case for all his colleagues, too, or they simply wouldn't have. No death is an accident. The soul—or oversoul, you might say—always knows what is best for its personality and strives to arrange those "fateful" events most constructive to the entity's overall growth.

The type of life we have just described with James' case is interesting to me. It's rather like a sideline among main occupations. No personality would look back, saying, "That was my best life!" But it did serve its intended purpose. It was a calming period in the physical world, a time of emotional retraction almost, a conserving or holding back of psychic energies; a life without great passion, heights of joy or sorrow, a life without peaks or valleys, for the most part smooth sailing. It was an effective counterpoint to James' other lives, which had been much more vital. It helped him get his bearings and reflect on what his next best course would be. After that somewhat reclusive life, he next threw himself into the fray with a passion for achievement and communication. With his next life he reached new heights.

7 | FRENCH COBBLER
Bigotry

WILLIAM was a cobbler in 18th century France. He lived in a rural village, enjoying a relatively simple life. He was aware of the extravagant goings-on of the elegant Paris set and was pleased to be far removed from those charades, nestled in the French countryside. The Parisians would have called William provincial, but he felt his life was the more complete. He viewed the lavish expenditures of the courtly life as wasted resources. He was thrifty to the core. Every scrap of leather, every bit of paper or metal, wood or rubber could be saved for some useful purpose. Today, you would say he believed in and practiced recycling. In those days, such a person was called penurious.

As you might guess, William the cobbler was a bit of a bigot. He felt superior to the grand city folks by his propensity to rate his country values over the urban lifestyle. There was a germ of truth in his observations, but not to the extent he carried them. He considered himself to be made of superior stuff compared to his city neighbors, actually reversing what he thought was scorn Parisians felt for provincials.

Even in his life his bigotry haunted him. William had a beautiful daughter who was courted by a Parisian gentleman who wished to marry her despite her lack of a fine dowry. Because of the obvious advantages of the match, William had to swallow his pride and his bile toward the fancy young man and allow the marriage. This caused him much pain; he felt slighted, even cheated, to have his own flesh and blood convert to the decadent lifestyle he had so long scorned. He retained this bitterness to the end of his life. At that time he had some difficulties to overcome on this side because of his harsh judgments of others.

Now, the reason I have chosen this story is because, whether you are aware of it or not, your current society has elements just as disparate as pre-revolutionary France. There are many post-hippie types who scorn lavish lifestyles, desire to have a simpler life, return to the earth, who spend their money judiciously and are more concerned with causes than with personal consumption.

While on the surface this latter group sounds like it represents a fairly healthy orientation, I mention this example because there is a kind of bigotry that exists nonetheless. Many tend to feel anger and resentment toward those who have wealth, judging them harshly. They assume that all the wealthy are selfish and self-indulgent.

Yet they are not qualified to so judge other lives. This is the same problem we have mentioned before. One sex is not superior to another, nor one race, nor one economic group. Personal worth resides in the heart where it cannot be easily observed by another. It is not necessary to say this, but I will say it anyway. There are many, many "rich" people who are good-hearted, extremely generous and wise souls. Their economic wealth is matched by their spiritual wealth. There are also wealthy people, of course, for whom this is not the case, but that is true of every classification of people you can name. By the same token, there are many post-hippie types, who choose a life of near-poverty, who are poor in spirit, who judge others of contrasting lifestyles harshly, asserting that theirs is the only way, the path of righteousness. Of course, there are many others in this category who are good-hearted and fulfilled.

I hope my point is clear. William the simple cobbler held some personal views which were not incorrect in themselves but were so rigid in his mind that they colored his views of all people. He tried to categorize others in order to fit them into his philosophy. By his reckoning, all wealthy Parisians were decadent and evil.

Circumstances in his own life were arranged so that he might reconsider this entrenched attitude, at the time his own daughter joined the ranks of the so-called decadent. This could have helped William reexamine his beliefs. Instead of growing out of his narrow-mindedness, however, William merely became more confused, bitter and resentful.

He paid dearly for it on this side, and he has had to devote an entire life to resolving the discrepancy. In his next life he was born into a wealthy family and strongly urged by his oversoul to reevaluate his lingering biases. He has met with some disapproval from others for his inherited wealth and has dealt with his confusions from this opposite angle. He has progressed well and, interestingly, suffered quite a bit, too. He was born to an especially stern father who stressed the accumulation of wealth above all else in life, and for many years William obediently accepted this teaching, despite a sense of uneasiness. Now he is reaching the end of his years—he is still incarnate—and he has achieved a balance in his own perspective by generously sharing his wealth where he feels there is need. Thus he is comfortable in his own attitudes about sometimes-conflicting material and spiritual elements.

	POLISH MILKMAID
8	**Kindness to Animals**

MOLLY was a milkmaid on a farm in 18th century Poland. We are not stuck in that century, as my secretary suspects. We simply can find another lesson in a life that happened to occur in those days. Life on the farm was arduous, as such a life still is, long and unceasing in its daily chores. Milk cows do not take vacations; they need to be milked twice a day, month in and month out. Molly was a cheerful and sturdy soul who enjoyed her earthy work and interaction with the animals. She didn't mind the burden of continuous labor. She worked for her family, who owned the dairy farm, and as she grew older she never married but instead continued her farming work to ever greater degrees. The family raised pigs, and Molly tended to them as well, plus sheep and chickens.

The farm was prosperous, but Molly became ever more pivotal to its smooth running by her instinctively correct and nurturing relationship with the animals. In other circumstances, this kind soul might have become a veterinarian. As it was, she was born into circumstances which helped her fulfill the purposes her greater soul sought—a close relationship with the animal kingdom, even to the exclusion of human relationships.

You may wonder what lesson this little tale holds, for Molly's life was devoted not so much to helping other people, although she was kind and generous, but to helping animals stay healthy and content in the farm setting.

The purpose is to show that human kindness can be expressed in many ways, and the opening of one's heart that we have urged on our readers has many possible manifestations. To aid the animals which surround one and with whom man shares the Earth is as noble as to help other people. Although the spirits of animals are not as complex nor developed as man's, yet animals have vital consciousness and a wide range of emotions that correspond closely with man's own emotional reaches.

Another reason for this story is to create a circumstance where we can describe, at greater length than a mere mention, the different kinds of experience that animals have on Earth. There are many misconceptions in your world about the animal kingdom.

First of all, animals do not contain spirits that were formerly humans. Animals are not the same in the spirit realms as human beings. Their consciousness and that of humans are not interchangeable; like water and oil, they won't ever mix. They naturally separate themselves into different experiences.

As Judy already has discovered in her study of other metaphysical sources, many animals from your realm are what are called "fragment personalities." These are partially-formed personalities which seek to remain in touch with the Earth and are connected with higher-developed collections of entities in Realms Five or Six.

The mind of the animal is very vital and has many similarities to yours but also huge chasms of differentiation from human mental life. The animal, for instance, has no language and does not see across its mind the endless chatter of thoughts the way people do. The animal's physical senses, however, are more acute and create a more intense interaction with its physical environment than a human feels. The animal is more at one with nature in this regard, in that animals are naturally intuitive—you might even say clairvoyant. They perceive the many small spirits of the natural world which dance about the countryside and of which you human beings are almost completely oblivious. Animals sense these spirits, interact to a small degree with them, and are generally more attuned to the close tie between the natural world and the invisible world of spirit which lies beneath it.

Yet animals have emotions and emotional needs much like people do, as any pet owner knows. These emotions can be pampered and improved by a loving relationship with people. In fact, there are many animals who enter your world with the express purpose of interacting with humans. Pets are one example of such personalities, and domestic animals, of course, are another. These "fragment personalities" enter the earthly realm knowing they are entrusted to the care of humans and seeking that interaction.

Molly's tender care of many domestic animals was a true response of her heart to the needs and desires of the creatures.

My secretary wonders about another aspect of this topic: do animals, like humans, enter this world to learn lessons, to grow spiritually? The answer is no. They enter merely to take a break, you might say, from the spirit realm, to be refreshed by the vitality of physical life and the physical Earth plane. It is an experience that is enriching but not really necessary to spiritual growth. They also enter in a thrust of comradely spirit and with a sense of helping to add to the beauty and wonder of the Earth. They enter because the hearts of people seek companionship on Earth in great variety.

There are other aspects of animal consciousness which are fascinating and which we haven't the space or time to cover here. Judy wonders about the smaller consciousnesses, like insects, and I am choosing not to comment on those now. But she has another question—the occasional vicious animal which attacks humans—and that question I would like to address.

The animal instinct is good, true and in tune with higher forces, yet there are occasional aberrations which appear in your world. A vicious dog, for instance, which attacks children is an example. This is difficult to explain. There are confused spirits which sometimes hover around the Earth plane and make their presence known. People think that they themselves can be "possessed" by evil spirits, but this cannot happen without their own assent at some level. Each person's oversoul is both powerful and good, capable of great help in directing one's life.

In the animal kingdom, however, the animal's connection to its source is sometimes a bit more tenuous. Animal instincts are stronger in some than others. Now and then a confused human-type spirit entity coexists for a time in an animal's body and causes troubling behavior. Usually such coexistence is denied from this side, but occasionally it is allowed to happen in order for a troubled spirit to sense the vitality of the animal's mind. In such rare cases, there is allowed a certain freedom of action, and if there is a tendency to viciousness, then that human spirit entity is not allowed on the Earth plane for a long time to come. As you can see by this explanation, temporarily inhabiting animal consciousness is on a rare basis a kind of early testing ground for troubled souls.

Other than those cases, the entities who enter animal consciousness emerge from the higher realms and are good to the core. They are animals, nonetheless, and they are endowed with a set of instincts, just as people are endowed with their human characteristics. Animals are also individuals and act accordingly. Judy has heard from Af that her black labrador, Rosie, is a fragment personality of Af herself. Yet, as Af explained, Rosie is her own dog. She will not disappear at death, or merge all out of recognition by joining Af. She remains distinctly herself yet does indeed join the larger entity of Af. This enriches Af's gestalt of personalities and is a beloved link with Earth life. [Rosie has since died. —J.L.]

These ideas are difficult to explain in a few words. The purpose in conveying them is to emphasize the desirability, from a spiritual viewpoint, of respecting animals' experience and offering love and support to animals as well as to humans. A life such as Molly's can be rewarding in this task.

<table><tr><td>9</td><td>

SCHOOLMARM
Close-Mindedness

</td></tr></table>

JANE was a school mistress in 19th century United States. A high school teacher, she had three children of her own and was very devoted to her students. Yet she felt that grades were the measure of accomplishment and that creative ideas were out of place. This attitude tended to make her overly strict. In other words, she believed strongly in the conventional wisdoms of the day and taught them as gospel. Students were not allowed to question facts, and Jane did not encourage original thinking. She adhered to her conservatism in all aspects of her life and did not change this straight and narrow path until she reached this side. She was shocked to see the truth.

The moral of this story is a universal one, for there are always many people in every society who ardently believe whatever are the accepted dictums of the time. This strict adherence to the popular view of reality is a shame, for it instills rigidity in the mind and spirit and crowds out the natural source of truth which is always gently present in one's inner life, available through the intuitions.

Therefore, despite our Jane's devotion to her students and their learning, her own narrow mentality actually thwarted many students and produced a joyless learning environment. It was a sad waste of daily opportunity to enrich the lives of others. Jane's rigid mind-set did not allow the expression of warmth and humor to be conveyed to her charges. She felt that education was not intended to be fun, that it was rote and must be force-fed to generally unwilling young people. This attitude itself created a certain reciprocal unwillingness in the students, as they sensed from her that their lessons were dull and rote.

So Jane's was a generally unfulfilled life, without joy or spontaneity. Her underlying goodwill, the driving force behind her desire to teach, was so shrouded with feelings of solemn duty that her spirit in that incarnation never really blossomed.

What might this mean to a modern reader? On the surface, the puritanism of those days has been left by the wayside, yet there is a basic lesson which is pertinent to all periods of history. It has to do with state of mind. To be openminded is also to be open-hearted. An open mind admits that one does not necessarily have all the answers to life and, too, that one is interested in the thinking of others. To be rigid of mind is to be egocentric, to believe that you yourself have all the answers, that you understand the secrets of the universe and that, if you might be proven wrong, you would simply rather not hear about it. You are comfortable clinging to your beliefs and prefer not to be bothered with contrasting ideas.

"You would laugh if you could see the hundreds of people appearing in these realms every day who will not believe where they are."

This little synopsis has meaning for nearly all people. It is natural to hold onto beliefs one has collected or developed over the years. My hope in telling the story is to shake you from the desire to hoard beliefs. Mental rigidity spoils many lives, and when souls appear in the spirit realms, this same rigidity presents many obstacles to growth.

You would laugh if you could see the hundreds of people appearing in these realms every day who will not believe they are where they are—in a world of spirit. They do not believe in a world of spirit; therefore it must not exist. But in fact it does and here they are! What a time our gentle counselors on this side have with convincing these dullards that they need only to pinch themselves and look around to see that their beliefs are mistaken!

Why is there this tremendous reluctance to alter beliefs? Partly it is due to the popularity in your time of dismissing the existence of the spiritual side of humanity and defining life by the physical world. This leads men and women to define themselves by their bodies, their ages, their jobs, their possessions. They do not see that their own spirits transcend all these temporal elements of life. By too closely identifying with the physical world, the true appreciation of life—the loving interaction of souls with each other and with the spirits underlying the Earth itself—is lost by the wayside. One never ponders or reflects on life's meaning, but adds up with a calculator the sum total of one's worth by adding the physical elements. The wealthy appear to be the most wise, the venerated. The poor and uneducated are lowly and despised. The man or woman who espouses common wisdoms of the day is the most trustworthy and stable of society's members. These are the people who have such a difficult time over here. They are like plow horses with blinders on, except that they love their blinders and are frightened of the entire horizon.

I hope through this story to awaken a few readers to their own shortcomings, if they can be honest enough to own up to a fault.

By correcting such attitudes on Earth, they will accomplish spiritual growth that would be very slow and difficult on this side.

It's hard to explain why growth is faster on the Earth plane, but I'll try. When people first find themselves over here, they have some instant insights and clairvoyant abilities. These are inherent to the spirit yet are hidden from you when you enter each Earth life. To understand the obvious truths is no great accomplishment and does not require exceptional abilities or effort. But if one can recognize truths while on Earth, where they are hidden, this does require exceptional effort, ability and desire. The physical world is like a mask which covers universal truths. Its purpose is a grand one: for people to learn to know themselves, behind their masks, for character to be tested and challenged, that is what physical life is all about. It is a magnificent opportunity for each individual to know himself or herself better, to learn to love other people despite the natural urge to be selfish. Life is a challenge to faith, to have faith that there are great and good purposes which people cannot understand, but which underlie their existence with greater security than the earth beneath their feet.

Our Jane did not find herself in Realm Two, because her life's accomplishments had not been that meager. But her experience on this side was full of frustration and discomfort for a long time. She yearned for a speedy return to Earth in order to undo some of the harm caused by her poor attitudes. She waited her turn, as all here do, and in time she was granted the privilege to be reborn.

In her next incarnation she chose circumstances to aid in developing an open mind. She was born to parents with different nationalities, who each spoke a different native language and who came from differing religious backgrounds. This was an early incentive to be aware of alternative approaches to life.

She later became a teacher, as she was before, but in this life she taught comparative religion, through which she developed a fundamental respect for differing ideas about life, God and the human spirit.

106

ENGLISH SERVANT
10 | Status Addiction

SARAH worked for a large household in England at the turn of the 20th century. She was married with two grown children at the time she advanced to her eventual post as cook. Among servants, this was a coveted position and one with a certain amount of prestige.

This is something of an "upstairs/downstairs" story. In fact, you would say the servants of that period were much more class-conscious that those they served, and this may perhaps be the rule. As the underdogs, they yearned for some measure of prestige and sense of worth in their community.

Sarah had reached her goal in her career when she became head cook. She did a creditable job, preparing marvelous meals and taking much pride in her work. If anything, she took too much pride, often identifying her personal worth with the quality of her cooking. Too, there was a certain ruthlessness which crept into her mind as she reviewed her career, for she felt it was necessary that she herself excel over others in order to attain her goals. This gave her a tendency to coldheartedness toward those around her, many of whom she knew to be somewhat envious. Overall, her life had a tone of a strong drive for ego gratification and an uneasiness which accompanied her attainment of the highest position she hoped for.

What on earth could this story mean to a reader in modern America? There is no longer a caste system; there are few servants; no one is driven to become a household cook.

But there is much striving in your society for prestige and exalted job status. That comparison is eminently clear. In fact, almost everyone attaches a great measure of personal worth to their occupation. This tendency is most unsatisfactory from a spiritual viewpoint. It creates the worst kind of discrimination by attaching value to higher job status and salary and considering lower positions or unemployment demeaning.

So our Sarah is an apt symbol of the embracing of this false system of values. As we have been teaching, each person ought to seek his or her own best path to fulfillment. In many instances this occurs by an individual making material sacrifices for what the heart urges, such as taking a position which pays less but offers more creative latitude or satisfaction. Or taking a certain line of work which is without much prestige in order to fulfill one's heart's desire.

Sarah succumbed to the poor thinking of her society by relating her own worth to that of her job. She felt overly proud and harshly judged others. This was very detrimental to her spirit and caused much unhappiness and discomfort both to her and those who surrounded her. In effect, she shut off her heart to her fellowman in her attempt to become exalted. The result was the opposite of what she had hoped for. She became smaller spiritually and retarded her own growth. This was apparent both in her world and in the spirit world to which she eventually returned.

This phenomenon is one of the most common maladies, certainly not limited to the serving class of England. You call it competition, and you consider the competitive spirit an integral part of the well-rounded person. The propensity extends beyond individuals to huge collections of persons, from schools and counties to states and nations. In its larger form it creates wars by the intense nationalism or patriotism which people espouse as a virtue but which only is a guise for the same pervasive evil, the "I am superior to you" complex.

Oh, how we weary of that attitude! We of the spirit realm who see the great truths about your world, we wish you could plainly see the folly of your own competitive spirit. That idea does so much damage to so many! Its underlying assumption is totally false—that there is not enough wealth or enough food to go around, that one must fight with others in order to achieve abundance or security. In a very basic sense the spirit of competition reveals a weakness in religious orientation, a lack of faith or sense of higher purpose. It springs from the lower reaches of human mentality; even the animal kingdom does not embrace a sense of necessary antagonism. For the most part, animals know by instinct that there is enough for all and that they can safely share their plenty. We wish humankind would listen to its own corresponding instinct.

A certain competitiveness in sports is not quite the same as this competitiveness in careers. They both do spring from the same strong urge to appease the ego, to set oneself above others. Like good coaches, we urge you all to be sportsmanlike in your lives. To be happy for your fellows when they succeed, even if you do not. To give others a chance to succeed, even if it means you must step aside. To see yourself as a part of a team of humanity, not as individual stars. The many who seek to shine brightly on Earth will find their circumstances dimmed on this side.

Such was the case with poor Sarah, who landed in Realm Two after her physical death. For a long time she had no inkling of why she was in such a dreary environment. Little by little she came to the awareness of how she had created her own poverty by striving to set herself above others.

In her next life she chose to be a simple farmer's wife. She worked hard, had little prestige in a culture which worships technology, learned to sense the abundance of the earth, the endless seasonal cycles of harvesting, resting over winter and planting anew. Her life has had much greater bounty for her spirit in its satisfaction of serving others and caring for the earth.

11 | MODERN CARPENTER
Loneliness

RICHARD is a carpenter living today. He enjoys his craft and does excellent work. In his relations with people, however, he does not have the same smooth competence. He feels awkward and lonely. He is lacking in confidence and worries over others' impressions of him. And so he has no lasting relationships and has remained unmarried well into his 30s. His life is somehow incomplete and he senses his own loss. He lives his life in solitary; he is waiting for life to happen to him.

I choose this example to illustrate a fairly common condition in your society: it is a condition of loneliness which is caused by the false assumption that individual people stand alone, that they are not connected to others. It is a false perception created in a person's head which carries no real truth. It is disorienting.

Men, women, the Earth and the spirits of the universe are all connected to one another. Each individual has unseen but real ties to his family, to others around him, to many spirits from my realm who monitor his earthly activities, actions, thoughts and progress, and who attempt to favorably influence him through his thoughts and intuitions. There are many who are intensely interested in each person's welfare.

Richard has deluded himself in his loneliness. He is not alone. There is a web of psychic and spiritual elements which supports him. Are his dreams not always there for his benefit, night after night? Do the thoughts running through his head ever cease, like a water tap turned off? His dreams and his thoughts are always there, a fertile, creative abundance for his own benefit. If he consciously chooses to ignore the lessons of his dreams and reject the helpful and true thoughts which spontaneously come to him, then he is free to do so. In that way he may work against his own best interest.

What should Richard do? How can he improve himself? Here

is a suggestion: he should rise out of himself, grow beyond his own egocentricity. He is no longer an adolescent and does not need to feel self-conscious in the presence of others. He can allow himself to take an interest in others, to open his heart to their realities—their interests, ideas and life circumstances. By truly caring for others he will be loved in return to a far greater degree than he would ever find with his current focus on himself alone.

In every life the individual is presented with opportunities to help others—on a bus, a city street, in the market, the neighborhood, in a multitude of small daily, common occurrences. These small and fleeting relationships are important to you, for they set the tone of all your relationships.

You can test yourself by asking such questions as: 1) Am I kind to strangers in an elevator or on the street? 2) Do I respond courteously to others? 3) Am I sensitive to the emotions of passing people? 4) Do I offer polite help where it is needed, such as when driving, walking or in other instances? Your answers to these questions will give you a clue about all your relationships, with family, business acquaintances and friends, too.

If you are curt, cold, aloof, superior-acting to strangers, you probably are less than a loving mate to your spouse, a truly caring parent, or a warm and sincere friend.

From this side we urge you all to shed your protective shells of loneliness and reach out in kindness and sympathy to all those who surround you.

12 | SECRETARY Career above All

DENISE was a secretary in the U.S., establishing her career in the late 1940s. The war was over and she sought for herself a secure life. She worked in a steel manufacturing plant for an executive and she felt that her job was an excellent one. Eventually she married, but she continued her career and did not have children. Her horizon was a narrow one, and for what she desired to accomplish in her life, she succeeded. Her goals were hollow ones from a spiritual viewpoint because they focused on job status and ego gratification above all else. She admired her boss but was uncaring toward many others around her. Work was her whole life; her husband, home and personal friends only represented the machinations of living for her.

This story sounds somewhat familiar to us, since we have covered similar terrain in various other accounts, but I bring it up for several reasons.

Primarily I mention Denise because U.S. society of the 1980s is very concerned with sexual identity, equality, and feminist rights. In her time, Denise was a women's liberationist in that she chose the very untraditional course of a career in business over a home life centered around children. After World War II, many ideas were starting to change about the traditional role-playing of the sexes.

My summation: it is good to be aware of sexual discrimination, but even better to be unaware of it where it does not exist. I can hear the outcry, "But it does truly exist today. Just look at salary statistics. Men are much higher paid even now."

The problems we see with abiding concern in such a cause as women's rights are these: it masks the greater realities and tends to align energies in that unproductive mode of "I want more for myself" rather than working toward giving more to others. I don't dispute there are inequalities relating to your sexes, but I do dispute the importance of protesting these inequalities. In many instances, they will be naturally self-correcting.

"It is foolish to feel that men and women are a breed apart. You all come from the same mold."

Let me put these comments in perspective. Although certain scientific and psychological tests show marked differences between men and women, it is foolish to feel that they are a breed apart. You all come from the same mold. The spirits of men and women are truly interchangable. There are subtle psychological and less subtle physical differences, but these are purely surface phenomena and not related to the deeper psychic identities that all people possess. By highlighting the differences, the disparities, you create rifts. You increase the false perception of men and women as identities somehow foreign to one another. The sexes were created, you might say, by God for the purpose of sexual interaction, love and reproduction. Period. The sexes are meant to draw men and women into love relationships with one another, to better explore and experience their own humanity. They are not meant to divide you from one another. You are not different creatures who think differently and have different needs.

This case is like the many other artificial divisions we have touched upon in this modest book. Men and women have in common their humanity and their spiritual purposes in physical life. The same is true of the various races, creeds and nationalities. This is an essential lesson to all people. All the Earth's creatures—humans, animals, plants, rocks—have a commonality of purpose and shared Earth life. (Even rocks live in their own way!) It is most important that people feel a brotherhood and sisterhood between one another the whole Earth over. Do not feel jealous of your colleagues who are male, while you are female, and who earn more money. Remember that true worth resides in the heart, and that you alone are responsible for your worth. It cannot be bestowed by an employer.

Remember, too, that job status is absolutely illusory. It means nothing to us on this side. In fact, we are saddened by the many souls who are led astray by their concerns over career position and prestige. Denise was just such a soul, and there are souls innumerable in your society who fall into that trap. Their goal in life is to attain dramatic success and perhaps wealth in their careers, to be admired by others for their achievements, to protect themselves from obscurity or a sense of mediocrity. These are all urgings of the ego, not the heart.

Man's ego has developed into a very strong entity for several reasons. In order to bring about your technological advances, your race chose to shut out certain portions of the intuition and to develop the "logical" mind to a greater extent. Ego was pushed forward in this process, in order for individuals to feel sufficient desire to accomplish their technological goals. These accomplishments are focused on the physical, material world. Largely ignored is the spiritual world, equally real, but less perceived by people who expend great energy on the material.

"It doesn't take great intellect to see that peace cannot be attained through arms buildup and military threats."

The ego will become humankind's enemy unless it is balanced by a redeveloped sense of the spiritual world. Strong egos divorce people from one another. Every time you lend a hand to another person and open your heart to another person, you momentarily set aside your own ego and focus your concern away from yourself. This is the true potential for progress of mankind, not in reaching the moon or making a better mousetrap.

Technological progress has its purposes, it is true. I will tell you what we understand of these purposes. Your technologies have developed in order to more clearly define what are the great concerns of your day. A facility in manipulating the physical world has not added to the true happiness of people on Earth; it has only added confusion. These confusions have almost always been a part of physical life. In a sense, the shortcomings of your sciences and industry have been brought to a head with nuclear technology. Now your race must ask itself the important questions which have been there all along. Is our nation superior to others? If we could, should we kill all members of another nation? Should we allow many of our country to die in a nuclear conflict? What is the meaning of war? Is there a way to avoid wars? Should we start thinking about the world in new terms? Aren't all people on Earth now connected to one another through this terrible technological power? Are there spiritual powers we have forgotten about? Is it possible to unite our entire planet in a sense of common purpose? Even if that possibility is remote, isn't it worth the try? Isn't the risk much less than the alternative risks of its opposite, international division and nuclear conflict? Shall we look for ways to attain peace on Earth?

Now, we have gotten apparently far afield from our little secretary Denise, but I see a direct connection. Denise represents in microcosm the individual's sense of separation in her striving for her own status above others. This symbolizes your nation's striving for similar status worldwide—to be the richest, the strongest, the most materially advanced. As you may be aware, these are false goals, false gods. As individuals and as a nation, you must divest yourselves of these goals and seek instead spiritual advancement and a joining of energies and goals with other nations. This alone will bring true happiness, personal satisfaction and worldwide peace.

Peace is never attained through war! It doesn't take great intellect to see that peace cannot be attained through arms buildup and military threats. Only a kind of stalemate based on fear is attained by those means, and that is the ultimate instability. Peace is based on trust, which requires honesty in word and action.

Your political leaders have truly reflected your society's thoughts and desires, so they are not to blame for your problems. As individuals and as citizens, you can now influence the trends in your country's government by communicating your ideas. On my side we see the tremendous power of the individual to influence others and to alter events. Rings of influence can be set in motion through one simple conversation. Be aware of your own power and use it wisely.

As for Denise, she suffered greatly when she reached this side, realizing that she missed all her major opportunities in life for spiritual growth. She has yet to return to physical life; she fears the shroud of physical life and the risk of missing life's lessons, but sooner or later she must brace herself and take the plunge. She will, by necessity, choose a path with some difficulties which may help teach her important lessons of humility and empathy for others.

13

FIELD LABORER
Contentment

ED was a field laborer in Mexico in the early 20th century. His life was a simple one of working the land on a large farm and cattle ranch of a prosperous family. He planted and harvested beans and other crops day in and day out. In certain seasons he helped tend the cattle. He had a wife and several children whom he loved dearly. Unlike many men of his society, he was not unfaithful to his wife but loved her passionately. He understood that most of his co-laborers felt much resentment in their lives; they envied the wealth of the ranch owners and they desired greater personal affluence. But Ed was happy, content in his heart and serene of spirit.

This story, which seems similar to several previous tales, is an example of an individual living a good and quiet life, with values far different than those of his countrymen. Because he was a quiet man, Ed's coworkers did not understand how his inner life differed from theirs, but his contentment was conveyed to those around him, and many benefited from his presence. He was not fashionable in his political ideas nor was he popular in his reticence to complain. Ed led no revolutions to alter his society.

He and his family were poor, but they had sufficient food and much love among them.

This does bear some relevant parallels to your society. There are those among you who quietly enjoy the life that others rail about, who give thanks truly for their daily bread and do not regret that they cannot afford motorboats or European vacations. They form no political constituency, but they go about their lives in a quiet contentment, conveying warmth and understanding to those around them. They do not yearn for the fast, rich life that is so extolled in your entertainment media.

As the time passes in the next 10-15 years, more and more people will enter this group of those who are happy with a simpler life. Families will join together to learn how to provide for themselves through farming and sharing. The current economic ailments of your country will actually encourage this wholesome trend, and more and more will look to it as an answer to their economic and social problems. As your society now stands, people are separated from one another and lack a sense of brotherhood with their fellows. When people, through mutual needs, are drawn together, the best of the human spirit can come forth. This will aid in the future changing social structures of your country and the rest of the world.

The time is drawing near that men and women from all over the globe must link their lives and their wills to avert nuclear war and to provide for one another. There is a mutual interdependence which must be recognized in order for your race to prosper.

14 | HAIRDRESSER
Modern Idolatry

JEANETTE is a hairdresser now living in your country. Jeanette is not her real name. She considers herself a beauty expert, and she concentrates all her energies on advising women how to become more attractive. The emphasis is on building self-esteem and also appearing attractive to men. She is fairly secure and content in her life and senses nothing major is lacking. Many women appreciate her advice, even eagerly seek it, although her major daily activity is simply hairstyling. She still tries to be aware of the "total woman," right down to the fashionable and complementary colors of the wardrobe.

I mention Jeanette as a contemporary personality so that the reader can easily identify with the subject of fashion. This arena touches almost all "civilized" cultures and causes much confusion and pain. In your society there is now unhealthy emphasis on physical attractiveness, bodily health, clothing, makeup and "projecting an image." These emphases are unfortunate for the reason that they are so much focused on benefit to oneself. To a smaller degree there is nothing wrong with wishing to appear attractive, desiring a healthy body, maintaining one's wardrobe; but the extent to which these interests are indulged has added to the problems of your society.

Certainly the worship of youthful beauty directly contradicts the idea of spiritual advancement. If your society more greatly regarded and recognized the soul or spirit, then the perfect youthful appearance so ardently admired would merely signal immaturity. The older members of your world would be more greatly sought after for advice and companionship.

My point goes beyond the youth-versus-old-age distinction. It goes to the sense of identity which people shape for themselves. It is natural, we know, for those personalities in physical bodies to identify with their bodies and their ages. But if they realized

RESENTMENT

that their souls transcend those aging, imperfect bodies, then there wouldn't be such a frenzy toward physical fitness and bodily beauty. People would be more aware of their inner life and more concerned with their relationships with others. Only by this type of change in individual attitudes will your society and your world be changed for the better. People cannot be drawn together in a spirit of mutual love and sacrifice when there are competitive games going on to be better dressed and more physically fit than the next person.

Again, I stress, I am talking about varying degrees, so a normal interest in one's own appearance and health is quite acceptable from the point of view of the spirit. But when one neglects home relationships to run 10 miles a day, for instance, or fusses endlessly over an extra 10 or 20 pounds of body weight, or buys enough clothing to clothe 10 people, then it becomes an obsession and interferes in normal human interaction. Then is the time to reevaluate one's orientation and begin looking to the inner, not the outer, life.

15 | OFFICE WORKER Resentment

CAROL is an office worker in modern U.S. society. She enjoys her clerical chores but finds much of her job to be unsatisfactory. She feels her salary is too low, appreciation from her superiors is insufficient and her fringe benefits are not broad enough. She harbors many resentments about her society. She worries endlessly about the problems of the day, especially the crimes of robbery and rape. She feels confusion about her own values and doesn't recognize the inherent contradictions.

She does not understand how she herself, Carol the ordinary individual, can make a difference in her society. She feels powerless to direct her own life or to influence other people. She

119

resents being a woman and feels that she has been discriminated against in her work.

What she doesn't see is this: that all people are joined together in an actual sea of humanity, like separate but united drops of water. All are connected and all influence the others. This is not empty theory. There are many people who, like Carol in this illustration, sever themselves emotionally from others, feel isolated and powerless, and so do a disservice to themselves and their culture.

The "criminals" so feared by many also feel isolated, confused and unloved. If they felt confident, loved and secure, they would not try to gain power by hurting or robbing other people. They would understand all power lies within.

What does this analysis mean to Carol? Simply this: she should rise out of her own loneliness and frustration and open her heart to others around her. Then she would feel she could affect her world, because other people would respond to her kindness. Her own power would increase as she exercised it. She would open her heart to the power locked within it, the proverbial power of goodness and love. This has a magical, expansive quality which increases as it is used. It is the cup which overflows, even as it is being drunk from.

If this happened, our Carol (now a hypothetically changed person) would find her personal attitudes and values had shifted. She would understand her own circumstances represented material sufficiency, that she had no cause for resentments, that her life presented her with many opportunities for personal growth and for expressing help and love to others around her.

Such attitudinal and philosophical changes would greatly enhance her own enjoyment of life. We wish there were more in your world who would open themselves up to their greater potentials, but too many are blinded by their conventional thinking.

16 | WEALTHY MERCHANDISER
Complacency

DAVID is a modern-day merchant—you call them merchandisers—who owns a large company which sells gardening supplies all across the nation. He is very prosperous, and his compnay is known for high quality workmanship in their products.

David has a family, a beautiful house, successful business and still he feels uneasy in his heart, as though something were missing.

He is open, warm and loving toward other people, so his spiritual health is in good order, yet he feels a void. That void is real; it comes from ignoring his deeper urgings toward helping other people. As a wealthy man owning a large and prosperous business, David is in a position of power. He has both wealth and influence behind him and therefore the ability to touch many others by his good example and action. Yet he has not stretched himself at all in those directions. He has funneled energy toward his own material comfort and that of his family. By so doing, he has made himself, his wife and children extremely "comfortable," with a secure financial future. But he has lost many opportunities to make some kind of self-sacrifice, even to a very small extent, in order to help others in their lives or endeavors.

What kind of help do I mean? Contributing time, money, business expertise, moral support, etc., to other individuals or organizations! David has behaved in a manner that is completely acceptable in your society. He has poured himself into his own business, made a success of it and lavished the fruits of that success on himself and his family.

How much better for him and his society if he had extended his horizons and reached out to help others in their lives and endeavors. His life has not been empty. He has made some strides by his kindness to his family and employees, yet how sad he didn't take his opportunities even further. We on this side feel sad, yet empathic, for such a person. Even though he will join those others who reside in the realms of light, yet he will deeply regret having bypassed some of his life's important lessons. What it means for his soul is the necessity of another entire physical life devoted to learning the same lessons his soul urged on him this time around. It's like flunking a grade and having to repeat the same subject a second year. It is lost time and lost opportunity—thickheadedness, you might say. And probably in his next life David will have greater obstacles to overcome to compensate for the easy material abundance in this life.

We on this side wish David would wake up and grasp life firmly by giving of himself to others and making certain sacrifices for his deeper ideals and spiritual goals. Only then will his soul become richer and will he actually progress as he ought to. Also, there are many people in your world who are ignorant of the greater truths of the universe, but who would learn quickly by good example. Why not set an example for them and for yourself? You've literally nothing to lose.

17 WAITER
Quiet Service

JASON was a waiter in a restaurant for many years. He just recently died and joined us in the realm of spirit. His life was fairly uneventful, and his personality was generally one of extreme humility. His job was to serve people. He considered himself inferior, both economically as well as by education. Yet he was honest, hard-working, warm and respectful of others. He was devoted to watching sporting events in his spare time, so he kept himself modestly occupied and entertained.

There is very little about this life to call attention to, and that in itself is the feature I wish to call attention to. Jason was so very ordinary in most regards that one wonders what his life was all about. He did not plunge the depths, apparently; there were no wild swings of passions, no bursting joy, no terrible despondencies, no gross misunderstandings of universal truths. We have a man who merely lived a quiet, uneventful life right up to his death.

"In the quiet living of physical existence, many men and women come to understand the most profound truths."

My aim in highlighting this life is to point out something obvious: many people of your realm and many of my readers might fit roughly into this category we define with Jason's example. They are living mostly ordinary, uneventful lives, wondering what it is all about. What I wish to say is this: each life has its purposes, and you are not to judge each other. Do not assume these quiet lives are without great meaning, for in the quiet living of physical existence, many men and women come to understand the most profound truths. These truths may only come to light for them after physical death, but their memories of life are vivid and impressive.

The truths which are often so well illustrated are these: physical life is a marvelous test to the spirit, it so completely takes on a guise, hiding its real purpose. It is like a costume party, but the guests have forgotten their underlying true identities and the test is an unspoken one of their need to identify their true selves beneath the costumes. The person who quietly accepts all that life offers, without great passions or questionings, is often the most surprised to see what lies beyond physical death. This surprise is a lesson in itself about physical life, and it is important to learn, because it helps the individual soul prepare for the next incarnation.

Many souls choose to be born into the physical world without truly understanding their tasks and limitations. So a quiet and uneventful life, which leaves less dramatic lessons to be learned after death, is often in itself an excellent lesson in the whole of physical life in general. Beware of judging others whose lives seem shallow to you. Each man and woman does indeed march to the tune of a different drummer.

18 | AUTO MECHANIC Learning through Craftsmanship

PAUL was a mechanic who died just recently. His life was spent working on the machinery of automobiles, repairing engines, with bolts, grease, transmissions, carburetors, and so on, the companions of his trade. He made a fair living and enjoyed pouring his energies into these machines. He had an excellent reputation for his careful and ethical work, and this was an additional satisfaction to him. He died before reaching old age and therefore avoided any prolonged physical ailment.

Like the last chapter, this life apparently is without radical swings of emotion or achievement. Yet it holds certain symbols for all to ponder. The focus on machinery is scorned by some in your society as artificial, inhuman, like rating computers over people. Yet there is nothing unnatural in man's affinity for the machines and technology of his own society's making. In fact, you would find similar interests in the spirit realm. Here there is no need for automobiles, of course, since travel is instantaneous, but there are many interests of a technical sort which are happily and fruitfully indulged in.

My reason for pointing out this life, because it so clearly

dwells on the material, the maintenance of automobiles, is to reaffirm the importance of not judging other people, by sex, nationality, age, religion or occupation. A fascination for machinery is a valid natural urging and very helpful to certain souls in their development. Paul, for instance, entered the realm of spirit having learned some excellent lessons from physical life. He understood intuitively that the spirit moves the physical world, not vice versa. His interest in machines was comparable to a physician's interest in bodies, simply to better understand the mechanism of movement and impetus. It's rather like a game of studying clockworks or jigsaw puzzles or even mathematical puzzles. This kind of intellectual stimulation and enjoyment is a part of life and existence.

My previous chapters have dealt, over and over, with the necessity and importance of interacting lovingly with other people, of helping others where possible. But many people do not aim most of their energies in this direction and do not need to. In Paul's case, he was fulfilling his deeper purposes by concentrating his energies on his craft. He was also warm, cheerful and friendly to the people he came in contact with.

By this example I wish to show that there are many manifestations of fulfilled lives, and once again to reiterate our main point. By following your heart's urgings, you will find your own best path. This should go in concert with, not against, your deepest yearnings. If you enjoy playing with computers more than anything else, then that is what you should do. Or repair cars. Or even race motorcycles. We must not judge others by our own standards for ourselves. Yet in all cases of human life, we must be aware of the importance of human sympathy and love. These are the greatest powers in your world and the greatest tools for your own fulfillment.

RUSSIAN LANDOWNER
19 | Adversity and Growth

BETH was a wealthy landowner in Russia before the Russian Revolution. Her husband was killed during the violence of the revolution and she fled the country. This was a time of tremendous lifestyle changes for the landed gentry and was both a shocking experience and a true test of human versatility. Beth came to the U.S., as did many of her fellow countrymen, and began a new life, a new beginning, in circumstances of near poverty.

I feel this is an interesting example for people today for several reasons. You, too, are living in a time threatened by war and violence on a more dramatic scale than ever before. This potential violence could alter your lives more drastically even than the example of Beth.

Beth symbolizes, much like the biblical story of Job, the age-old experience of spiritual and material adversity. After attaining great material comfort and wealth, to lose all, even one's loved ones, can truly test the spirit. The lesson one should learn is that the spirit is always there, that the spirit is the true foundation of life, that the spirit is the only true wealth of existence.

Beth graciously made her transition to a new life in the U.S., discovered her inner strength, and learned much from that particular incarnation. She suffered greatly, too, of course. But her life was beautifully fulfilled.

There is a deeper parallel here for your time than appears on the surface. Many in your society suffer as they experience the reduced economic circumstances arising from a worldwide recession. We watch these events with interest, and we see the broader strands of influence and patterns which cause such changes and which shape the future. We see that this withdrawal from the opulence of the past will continue rather than let up. There will be no return to the wealth of the 1950s. Many in your world even now can see the bright side of this trend, for there has been great waste of natural resources on Earth in order to support such affluence. The scarcity of energy sources will force your society to become restructured now along more humble, more appropriate lines compatible with the resources of the Earth.

It is time to turn away from the ardent materialism of America's recent history, which is simply based on self-gratification, and turn to developing greater spiritual strength and links with one another. In the end, this will prove most rewarding and enjoyable to all involved. There is no greater satisfaction, truly, than sacrificing one's own interest in order to share love and plenty with others. And a time of much greater sharing is coming near.

20 | TEACHER Losing One's Way

ELAINE is a teacher living today in the U.S. She finds certain basic ideals drew her into her profession early in her life, but in the interim she has grown disenchanted. She watched the tremendous buildup of affluence in the society, and she resented the lack of large salaries for teachers. The adequate pay she has received seems comparatively inadequate to her.

Therefore, as the years have gone by (she lives in Pennsylvania), she has lost interest in her real task of communicating with young people and has grown frustrated and bitter. She participated in recent wage strikes, but her higher salary did not increase her satisfaction. Satisfaction is a matter of the soul, and money does not touch that realm.

With the economic troubles of the country, Elaine is now more disconsolate and confused than ever. She sees her desired level of material affluence even further from reach, out of her direct control, and she doesn't know what she wants.

I give this life as our last example because Elaine represents the growing confusion, frustration and bitterness of so many.

Perhaps, reading this book, you have come to see the main thread which winds through it. You live in a physical world, a material world, but you are spiritual beings, with spiritual needs as pronounced as your physical needs. The test of physical life is to overcome the illusion that the visible physical world is all of life, and to welcome the intuitive, spiritual urgings which come to you as naturally as the urgings of your appetite.

Your failing economy and your strife in international relations are coming to a head. You can see chaos close by: on one hand, your economy verges on collapse; on the other, your country verges on the worst kind of idiocy, nuclear war.

These crises can be viewed as excellent opportunities. They will help to force you all to think hard about what you are doing. These events are not external events. They are not unrelated to you and the way you think. As long as you selfishly grasp at material abundance for yourself at the expense of others in your society, whether it is school children, other taxpayers, big companies or whatever entities you think of as the source of this abundance, you divide yourself from others and set a stage for conflict—economic, political, military, spiritual.

If you can follow the lessons of your heart instead of the "practical" lessons espoused by your sick society, then you can reverse these trends and find a future which does what you need done—provide material and physical adequacy for everyone; sustain a livable, renewable life cycle for all creatures of the Earth; and provide a world government for all nations to coexist in peace and respect for each other.

This last sentence probably sounds hopelessly idealistic, even utopian. But consider your alternatives—the ones which you face today. Those alternatives can destroy your planet and pitifully diminish the human spirit. If you cannot envision a peaceful and abundant future, then it will never come to pass. Yet if you can envision it, imagine it, then at the very least you can begin to take small steps toward it.

A first step is this: give of yourself to others. In this small way you can make a truly great contribution to your whole society. For each individual possesses great power of which he or she is totally unaware.

Next, you can try to envision a simpler life. Not one of poverty or need, but of less material abundance. Try to envision the way your grandparents lived as children. Move away from electric applicances. Think about simplifying your lives with fewer possessions, not more. By focusing less on possessions, you can focus more on human relationships. In this direction you will find greater satisfaction.

Try to learn some basic skills such as humans have practiced for centuries: vegetable and fruit gardening, basket weaving, hand sewing, simple cooking, domestic animal care, fabric weaving. These skills will be needed more as time goes on and can be productively shared with others.

Imagine how your life would be changed if basic services such as electricity and water were shut off. I am not making a prediction here, just urging you to think about alternative lifestyles. Try to feel more comfortable with the idea of self sufficiency. As human beings, you do not require indoor plumbing and electricity to survive. You do require water to drink, food to eat, shelter. These are the necessities of life. The material abundance you know has, in a sense, separated you from your true sense of your own humanity.

By evaluating basic needs and fostering your own ability to provide them for yourself, you can rejoin your sense of humanity. Too, be aware that by joining in a spirit of love and assistance with other people, you can protect each other.

Now, I am not suggesting an Armageddon is near. Nor do I suggest you all move to communes in the country. But we do see it will be necessary to reestablish your ties to the soil. If you have noticed, in your current economy, people both in the city and in the country are finding it increasingly difficult to live. City workers and farmers both need a new design for living.

If you have a yard, plant a garden and learn to preserve food. Share if you can with friends, neighbors or others of your community in need. If you have surpluses of anything, think about who would benefit by your sharing. Remember that others don't want charity, just a chance to make a living on their own. If you are a farmer, perhaps you could sublet a portion of your land to individuals to put in truck gardens. Look again at horses for farm help rather than the large, expensive, gasoline-run equipment. Think simple.

If electricity should fail, remember your life should not be a misery. Remind yourself of simpler ways to conduct household affairs. The sun each day brings light for your benefit. Lanterns are available for inside spaces—why not learn to use them safely? Wood-burning stoves are an asset, since they require a replenishable, fairly abundant natural fuel. [This is not the case everywhere. We should be looking seriously at environmentally sound alternative sources of energy.]

Some of your earthly experts are suggesting a return to small-scale farming as a solution to certain economic and social ills. We agree. Your dense urban areas have created much social sickness, and you should try to move back to the land, in small, self-sufficient communities.

All of these efforts we do not suggest be taken precipitously. But start to think about alternatives to your high-technology lifestyles and you will be imagining a future that is possible, that is self-sustainable and that can allow a return to the basic sense of spirituality that is humanity's birthright.

And all this advice is from an old ghost. With my warmest and deepest regards to you all.

—Your Bedouin Friend

The End

Index

Other Titles by
Judy Laddon

A Further Step Beyond The Veil
and
Another Twenty Life Stories:
Reminiscences From The Afterlife

Another Look At The Life Beyond
and
Twenty Life Stories Of Career Decisions:
Dedicated From The Afterlife By A Ghostly Bedouin

For additional copies of the above-listed
title combinations, send $7 each to:

Lawrence Shook Communications
4327 South Perry
Spokane, WA 99203

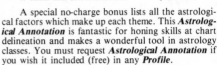